Old, Alone, and Neglected

Comparative Studies of Health Systems and Medical Care

Jeanie Schmit Kayser-Jones

Old, Alone, and Neglected

Care of the Aged in Scotland and the United States

UNIVERSITY OF CALIFORNIA PRESS

Berkeley • Los Angeles • London

University of California Press
Berkeley and Los Angeles, California
University of California Press, Ltd.
London, England
© 1981 by
The Regents of the University of California
Printed in the United States of America

1   2   3   4   5   6   7   8   9

Library of Congress Cataloging in Publication Data

Kayser-Jones, Jeanie Schmit.
    Old, alone, and neglected. Care of the aged
    in Scotland and the United States
    (Comparative studies of health systems and
    medical care)
    Includes bibliographical references and index.
        1.   Old age homes—United States—Case studies.
    2.   Old age homes—Scotland—Case studies. I.   Title.
    HV1465.K39   362.6'1'09411   80-19711
    ISBN 0-520-04153-4

For my grandparents, John and Anna Fohl,
my parents, Nick and Loretta Schmit,
and especially for my husband, Theo

Contents

Foreword

The nursing home is a burgeoning institution that has become our society's principal resource for long-term care for those we call the "frail elderly." These institutions, particularly those operated for profit by corporations or individual proprietors, have attracted the attention of both social critics and government representatives. Those who have traced the history of the nursing home industry fix the time of its greatest growth in the years just following 1965, when the advent of Medicare and Medicaid payments made it possible for the Federal Government to reimburse convalescent facilities for care of the disabled elderly. The funds paid to nursing homes rose from $1.3 billion in 1965 to $3.5 billion in 1972. By 1977 the total number of nursing homes was over 18,000, three-fourths of these being run for profit. Clearly, the nursing home industry is a big business in the United States, and with increasing proportions of older people it continues to expand.

One would assume, because of the scope of this institution in our society, that a great deal of research would have been conducted on their operations and their characteristics. Such is not the case; in comparison with research on acute-care hospitals, clinics, and other health facilities, research on nursing homes is sparse. Furthermore, such research as has been done has focused on two sorts of problems: first, there have been studies (sponsored in the main by federal agencies) of costs, profits, and standards; second, there has been some research by psychologists and other behavioral scientists on the impact of institutionalization on individual functions of residents—their morale, physical capabilities, memory, and the like. Economists have carefully examined the problems of costs of operation and also of regulation and standardization. Policy analysts have described the ways in which the enactment of public laws has served or mis-served the supposed recipients of tax-supported services, including long-term care. Sociologists and social critics have written about alarming deficiencies in safety standards, about debasing physical environments, about lack of proper regulation and oversight, about low standards and pay for staff.

To my knowledge, this book is the first full-scale anthropological study of nursing homes, and Dr. Kayser-Jones only the second anthropologist to conduct any ethnographic work within these institutions. She is perhaps uniquely qualified to conduct the research she reports here. First, as a professor of nursing, she brings to her work a breadth of knowledge about health, illness, and the organization of care that is rare indeed among social scientists. She constantly displays a sophistication and an acute vision of the old as patients and their needs for medical and nursing services, in both physical and psychological areas. Second, Dr. Kayser-Jones is also a medical anthropologist, and she has turned her knowledge of comparative methods in social research to her task here—to describe and explain the factors underlying the condition of elders in two nursing homes, one in the United States and the other in Scotland. This comparative view presents a completely new vision of the interrelationships between (1) the structural characteristics of the institutions and the cultural milieux within which they are set, and (2) the nature of human interrelationships fostered by the condition of life among the residents of such settings.

In her anthropological analysis of Pacific Manor, a nursing home in California, and Scottsdale, a geriatric hospital in the east of Scotland, she has utilized two models of behavior. First, she has concentrated on the social and economic machinery of the two institutions—how they are managed, staffed, and operated; how financial support is obtained; how they are perceived by patients, health workers, relatives, and community. This approach is a time-honored one in the social sciences, and it discloses many differences between the two institutions. Of particular note is the discussion of the ways in which historical factors have promoted institutions for care of the elderly in the United States that are largely cut off from meaningful contact with the other institutions that are most needed: the medical and nursing professions on the one hand and community residents on the other. The United States nursing home described here, Pacific Manor, is a virtual island in that residents are cut off in time from the important events, ceremonies, and people that once gave meaning to their lives and that seem to continue to do so at Scottsdale. They are cut off in space from the attentive physicians, the alert and well-informed nurses, who might detect reversible causes of decline and stop avoidable deterioration. They are cut off, as are so many in American life, from surrounding community activities and sometimes find themselves miles away from their home neighborhoods and their old friends; often they remain untouched by the social life that goes on around them.

Structural differences like these have been carefully presented here, but they are only a part of the picture Dr. Kayser-Jones has presented.

The second approach that Dr. Kayser-Jones has employed is that of process or interactional analysis. This is an approach that derives from the ethnographic field method. It requires long hours of "being there" in the role of observer with free access to the interactions and interchanges that take place among all kinds of actors in the setting observed. Careful ethnographic work makes it possible to understand not only the effect of structural characteristics on the nature of care, but also the symbolic values of seemingly minor elements of interaction in the total context of status, power, control, and service.

Dr. Kayser-Jones's use of interactional analysis enables her to address some of the most perplexing questions we have about nursing homes and the quality of life within them. For example, we know that, in spite of the fact that employees of nursing homes are notoriously underpaid and undertrained, some residents receive considerably better care than others. In the past we have only been able to speculate about the reasons for these differences. Through her meticulous interactional observations, Dr. Kayser-Jones has described the social drama of exchange relationships in new ways that disclose the linkages between certain structural forms and the conditions of life they generate. To provide only one example, Dr. Kayser-Jones's study of the process of gift and service exchange at Pacific Manor in comparison with that at Scottsdale demonstrates that availability of even meager resources for informal exchange with nonprofessional (and sometimes even professional) personnel has a direct bearing on the quality of service that an individual resident can obtain. Furthermore, this circumstance makes the petty theft and pilferage at Pacific Manor a fact of enormous importance to the informal exchange network that keeps the aged patient from complete helplessness and dependency. Nursing home administrators and health professionals may see the theft of a few dollars a month, a radio, a few garments, an occasional box of candy, as a small matter of concern, given the hundreds of thousands of dollars each year that they take in for long-term care. Dr. Kayser-Jones's analysis makes it clear that there are two kinds of capital in the nursing home—one is "big money"—the huge costs charged to the patient, the patient's family, or to the government; this money is not available to the patient in everyday negotiation for service. The second is "penny capital" or pocket money and goods over which the elderly patient has day-to-day control, and it is the latter (the small change, the cookies, the little gifts), not the unseen flow of money to proprietors, that helps older residents improve the services they receive in the nursing home. When theft is possible (and rampant because ignored), the last counters are stripped from those who must try to negotiate enhancement of the quality of life during their last years. Simple but critical differences between Pacific Manor and Scottsdale in this regard protect the elderly from total impoverishment. Scottsdale has a little "banking system," a small canteen, and a safe place to keep personal belongings; Pacific Manor does not. Dr. Kayser-Jones shows us how in the nursing home life hangs on small threads such as these.

In this work, Dr. Kayser-Jones concludes her discussion with the nature of three "institutional barriers to quality care." She lays the case of low-quality nursing home care directly at the feet of physicians and registered nurses, among whom she finds a default in leadership and responsibility. Secondarily, she discusses the nature of accountability in the American profit-making institutions, with its lines going to proprietors and regulatory agencies, and not to health professionals. Finally, she discusses the impact of the organization and financing of health care in the United States and the ways in which they lead to pauperization of the aged, even those who enter the nursing home system with substantial assets. This discussion is an eloquent plea to both health professionals and to those who influence health policies in our country to begin to consider major changes in the ways in which long-term care is provided. Otherwise, as Dr. Kayser-Jones has so clearly shown, the elderly who become ill and frail will remain neglected, exploited, and dehumanized; their wounds will be unbound, their cries for help unheeded, and their pain unrecognized. This volume will surely stand as one of the best evidences we have of the need for the development of humane and responsible geriatric care.

Margaret Clark

Preface

Old, Alone, and Neglected is concerned with the care of the institutionalized aged in the United States. It was written because I believe that, despite earlier reports of conditions in nursing homes, many Americans either are unaware of or refuse to acknowledge that many of the institutionalized elderly receive inadequate care and are often subjected to inhumane treatment during the last years of their lives.

Perhaps it is well that we do not know what lies ahead of us in our old age. However, this inability or reluctance on the part of the younger generations to consider the possible infirmities of old age may in part contribute to the problems encountered by the elders in our society. It seems that when we are young we cannot imagine that we will ever be old and helpless. As we reach middle age, we know intellectually that we too will become old. But at this period in our lives, surrounded by friends, involved in our work, and enjoying good health, we find it difficult to envision old age as a time when we may be devoid of friends and property, lonely, and dependent on others for care. Unfortunately, when old age is upon us, and if institutionalization becomes necessary, it is often too late to change the unpleasant conditions of our existence. So it is that when placed in an institution, some of the elderly cope with the hostile environment by withdrawing, others accept their fate with complacency, and a few display great courage and nobility in an effort to hold onto their individuality and humanity.

report we will

(In this ~~book I~~ have attempted to describe through the eyes of the elderly what it is like to be old, disabled, and institutionalized.) Through personal interviews with the aged, I have learned how it feels for them to be dependent on others for their basic needs and how dehumanizing it is to be deprived not only of essential care but of many of the amenities that give humaneness, warmth, and meaning to their lives. This book compares care in one institution in Scotland (which I shall call "Scottsdale") and one in the United States (which I shall call "Pacific Manor"). Scottsdale is a model institution in which the elderly appear to be content and happy, whereas at Pacific Manor the elderly residents express much discontent and unhappiness with their care.

It is now two years since I completed the research upon which this book is based, but I can still vividly remember my personal feelings when visiting the two institutions. I distinctly recall feeling happy each day as I went to Scottsdale to collect data; and when I left in the evening, I went away with a feeling of peace. I knew the elderly people were well cared for and basically content. By comparison, I found it difficult many times to continue my field work at Pacific Manor. As I entered the nursing home, I could hear some patients calling out for help; others, poorly groomed and clad only in brief hospital gowns, were restrained in chairs. Many would call to me for help, and consequently it took me longer to collect the data in the American nursing home. As a medical anthropologist who is also a nurse, I frequently had to step out of my role as a research scientist and attend to the needs of the elderly. On some occasions, conditions within the nursing home overwhelmed me and I had to leave and return another day. I can well imagine how painful it must be for families to visit their relatives and for conscientious staff to care for the elderly in such an environment.

I believe this book will be of interest to a wide audience, and it is my hope that it will be read by gerontologists, social scientists, health care providers, and those involved in health care policy at both the academic and governmental levels. Additionally, I hope that it will be read by students in the health and social sciences and by laymen as well. The impetus for change in institutional care may come only as a result of pressure from groups outside the health profession and from idealistic young students who will not be content with the present status of geriatric care in the United States.

The findings of this research, along with other research studies, provide us with solutions to many of the problems in institutional care of the aged. We have identified the problems, we have the resources, we need only the motivation to change the structures that will provide incentives to deliver quality care to the institutionalized aged.

The facts in this book are true; the names of people, places, and institutions have been changed. Additionally, specific details of the institutions and individuals have been modified to ensure anonymity.

Jeanie Schmit Kayser-Jones
San Francisco
May 1980

Acknowledgments

This book has evolved out of my doctoral research, which was supported by United States Public Health training grant GM-1224; I appreciate my appointment to the grant by Professor George M. Foster. I am also grateful to Professor Foster for his thorough reading of the manuscript, which resulted in numberless improvements and clarifications, and for his continuing efforts to convince me that in writing it is quality and not quantity that counts.

I owe my enthusiasm for gerontology to Professor Margaret Clark; she has given me continuing guidance and has offered invaluable insight into the analysis of the data. I shall always be grateful to her for being an unending source of inspiration, motivation, and intellectual stimulation.

I also wish to express my gratitude to Professor Elizabeth Colson, Dr. Fred Dunn, and Dr. Gert Brieger for their special concern, support, and encouragement, and for their valuable criticism of the manuscript.

The support and counsel of friends and colleagues stimulated me to write this book; nevertheless, this work would not have been possible without the cooperation of the wonderful old people at both institutions, the staff who facilitated the research, and especially Dr. Leslie Wilson, who made possible my research work in Scotland. I also want to thank the personnel in all of the geriatric institutions I visited in Scotland. I shall always remember their warmth, kindness, their enthusiasm for geriatric care, and the biscuits and lovely cups of tea they provided during each visit.

My interest in nursing home care goes back many years; and throughout those years, Mrs. Marilyn Fravel, a nurse (and former student of mine) who has dedicated all of her professional life to the care of the elderly, has aided me immeasurably and has continually facilitated my research work in nursing homes. The work I have done would have been far more difficult without her assistance, and I am grateful to her for giving so unselfishly of her time.

As a professional nurse planning anthropological research that could conceivably present health care professionals in the United States in an unfavorable light, I had some hesitation in approaching such work. I found little interest or encouragement from professional colleagues in my plans for research in nursing homes. Just when it seemed there were few, if any, physicians who were aware of or sympathetic to the needs of the institutionalized elderly, a physician-friend, knowing of my interest in gerontology, gave me a copy of *Why Survive? Being Old in America*, by Dr. Robert Butler. Dr. Butler's sensitive portrayal of old age in America and his courage in coming forth as a physician critical of the professional care of the elderly in the United States provided me with the resolve and determination to pursue my research goals. I should like to acknowledge that his book has been an important influence in my development as a gerontologist.

I especially want to thank my typists, June Richards, Joan Mello, Roxanne Kendrick, and Bella Khedr for their careful work in the typing of the manuscript. All of them worked under the pressure of deadlines, and without their assistance the book could not have been completed. I am also grateful to Dan Dixon of the University of California Press for his careful and thoughtful editing of the final manuscript.

On a more personal level, I want to thank my mother-in-law, Mrs. Charlotte Jones, for taking me in as one of the family, for providing me with warm, comfortable lodging during my stay in Scotland, and for tending to so many of my personal needs, thereby enabling me to carry out my research more expeditiously. I am also grateful to my brother-in-law and his wife, the Reverend Doctor and Mrs. Edmund S.P. Jones for their warmth and hospitality and for including me in many of the social and church activities in the community; these experiences gave me valuable insight into the Scottish culture.

I wish to extend a special and personal thank you to my parents, Nicolas and Loretta Schmit, for teaching my brothers, sisters, and me as children to love, value, and respect our grandparents and other elders, and for raising us in a home that exemplified that love and respect.

Many have contributed significantly to the completion of this work; however, without question, my deepest appreciation is to my husband, Theo. I wish to express a special acknowledgment to him for assisting me with my field work in Scotland, for spending countless hours with me as an empathetic listener, for knowing just how to lift my morale after a difficult day, and especially for his continuing belief in and support of my research and the writing of this book. I could not have continued without his loving support; no husband could have given more.

1

An Overview

This book offers an ethnographic cross-cultural comparative study of one long-term-care institution in Scotland and one in the United States. The purpose of the research was to investigate criteria for quality care for the institutionalized aged and to discover what institutional arrangements will encourage the maintenance of high standards of care. The current health care system in Scotland is basically the same as that in the rest of the United Kingdom, including the financing and delivery of health.care services—a major concern of this book. Although Scotland is only one part of the United Kingdom of Great Britain and Northern Ireland, the general statistics of the aged that I present and the description of the structure of the geriatric service apply to the entire United Kingdom. Hereafter, instead of using "United Kingdom" I shall use the more common terms "Britain" and "British," which refer to England, Scotland, Wales, and Northern Ireland.

The motivation to conduct the research that led to the writing of this book came from a number of professional experiences. As a nurse-clinician working in an acute-care hospital, I saw many elderly patients discharged to nursing homes only to return some weeks later with bedsores, pneumonia, or other conditions that suggested a lack of care. Later, when I began to teach in a school of nursing, my students who were employed in nursing homes (because one could always get a job there) frequently spoke of the low quality of care and remarked that they would never work in such an institution once they were registered nurses. Their comments made me curious about the conditions in nursing homes; and later as a doctoral student in medical anthropology, I soon learned that the elderly who were housed there were lonely, deprived, and neglected: many were receiving only minimal custodial care.

Although these professional experiences stimulated my interest in the care of the institutionalized elderly, I did not realize until later, while conducting the study, that the idea for this research was planted and began to germinate because of a personal experience many years before. One day, while collecting data in the American nursing home, I was asked by the staff to visit an elderly man whose wife had recently died. As I listened to his story, I found myself becoming more and more attached to him. He had immigrated to this country at the age of 20 and had become a successful businessman. He and his wife were childless; and since her death, unable to care for himself, he had been placed in the nursing home. After visiting this man several times, I realized that he reminded me a great deal of my grandfather, who had died ten years earlier in a nursing home, and my thoughts went back to that experience.

It was 1964, and I was a young head nurse working in a major teaching hospital in a large Midwestern city. Then, as is common today, I was one of the many health care professionals who believed that everything important in health care revolved around major, acute-health-care facilities. Although I had been a nurse for several years, I had never been inside the doors of a nursing home. One evening my mother called to tell me that my 94-year-old grandfather was no longer able to care for himself; because of failing health he had been placed in a nursing home. My grandmother had died 10 years earlier, and since her death my grandfather had staunchly remained by himself in their home. I went home that weekend to visit him in the nursing home. I was aware of a depressing environment and unpleasant odors as I entered the building and walked down the hallway to the room where my grandfather lay. The drapes were drawn; the room was quiet and darkened as if waiting for death's approach. I stood by my grandfather's bed and spoke to him, but he did not reply. His eyes were closed, and his demeanor was that of a person who had lost hope. This was so unlike my grandfather, who had been an extremely strong and independent man all of his life, that I could hardly believe he was the same person. Leaning over the bedside rail, I took his hand in mine, kissed him goodbye, and left the room, knowing that I would not see him again. He died that night.

I know now that my grandfather need not have died alone in that cold, impersonal, nursing home; yet today, even more so than a decade ago, elderly people are left to die alone and unattended in similar institutions. My grandfather was not impoverished or indigent, nor was he neglected and unloved by his family. An immigrant to this country at the age of 18, he had worked hard, acquiring substantial property before reaching old age. He was able to afford the best of care; but for the disabled elderly in this country there are few alternatives to institutional care, and among the available institutions there is often little choice.

In the intervening years, when I read or heard about the deplorable conditions in nursing homes in the United States, my thoughts often went back to my beloved grandfather as he lay dying in that nursing home. Thus it is not surprising that 10 years later, in 1974, when I considered various topics for research, I chose to focus on the problem of the care of the institutionalized aged.

The lack of adequate long-term-care facilities for the disabled elderly affects people of all income levels, of all races; it is present in every geographical area of our country. The problems of institutional care are especially traumatic for the aged poor, but I have learned from my research that even the middle and upper classes may not escape the indignities, the dehumanization, and the lack of medical care that is often found in institutions for the aged. Money cannot buy what is not available, and frequently institutions that have a fine reputation also have a 2-year waiting list; consequently, people are forced to accept what is available. What is available is often very poor institutional care.

The Problem

In 1870 only 2 percent of the population of the United States was 65 years of age and over; by 1970 the aged population had increased to 9 percent (Cowgill 1974), and it is predicted that within the next few decades the aged will constitute 15 percent of the population (Leaf 1973). There has been a sizable increase in life expectancy since the beginning of this century; it has risen from 49 years in 1900–1902 to 71.9 years in

1974 (Siegel 1978). Life expectancy is usually calculated not only at birth but at each age as well. The greatest gains in life expectancy between 1901 and 1959 have been at the younger ages (1–25 years), while the gains at the older ages (55–75 years) have been small. For example, at age 1 the gain in years was 15.3; at age 5 it was 11.8; and at age 25 it was 8.6 years. By contrast, the gain at age 55 was 3.2 years; at 65, 2.2; and at 75, 1.6 years. Although the gains at the older ages were small in absolute terms, they have resulted in a dramatic increase in the proportion of people over age 65 (see Table 1). Advances in science, improvements in public health, the dissemination of health education, and the application of technology to the control of mortality and fertility are some of the factors responsible for the increasing numbers of aged people in our population.

Although science has succeeded in extending the life expectancy of man, it has not been as successful with the medical, social, and cultural problems that accompany old age. One problem is the institutionalization of chronically ill elderly people in convalescent hospitals and nursing homes. On any given day over one million people 65 years of age and older currently live in various types of institutions. Moreover, with advances in cardiovascular and other medical research, the life expectancy of Americans will continue to rise, and in the future there will be even more older persons than there are today who will need to be institutionalized with multiple, chronic illnesses. In fact, it is estimated that 20 percent of the present elderly population will require at least some institutional care during the balance of their lives (Butler 1975).

The prevailing quality of institutional life for the aged in the United States is largely negative. Studies have reported on the shocking conditions in many nursing homes in the United States (e.g., Henry 1963; Townsend 1971; Mendelson 1974; Butler 1975; Moss and Halamandaris 1977). Some of these studies have investigated the effects of institutionalization in general and speak to the depersonalizing effects of institutions (e.g., Bennett 1963; Coe 1965; Kahana 1973); others have concentrated on mortality rates and the effects of relocating the aged from the community to an institution and from one institution to another (e.g., Camargo and Preston 1945; Costello and Tanka 1961; Aldrich and Mendkoff 1963; Killian 1970; Markson 1971; Boureston and Tars 1974; Tobin and Lieberman 1976; Pino, Bosica, and Carter 1978). Few studies, however, have focused on the quality of care in long-term-care institutions for the elderly; Kosberg (1973), Kahana (1973), and Anderson (1974) all agree that there is a lack of knowledge of what constitutes quality or effective care. Townsend (1962), in an extensive study of institutions for the aged in England and Wales, attempts to measure the quality of care; and Henry (1963) describes, compares, and analyzes the conditions and poor quality of care in three institutions for the aged in the United States.

Rationale for a Comparative Study

Demographic Characteristics

The rationale for a comparative study to help find answers to American problems lies in the fact that, although their demographic characteristics and the needs of their elderly appear to be similar, Britain and the United States have followed rather different paths in attempting to cope with the dilemma of the institutionalized aged.

In both countries the numbers and proportion of elderly persons continue to rise steadily (see Tables 1 and 2). Also, the life expectancy for men and women in the two countries is very similar (see Table 3). However, the increase in life expectancy at birth over the past decades in both Britain and the United States has been greater for women than for men. Mortality rates of males in both countries, throughout the age scale and for all the leading causes of death, are well above those of females; this has resulted in a disproportionate number of older women in both countries.

The number of very old people is increasing dramatically in both countries. In Britain it is predicted that from 1975 to 2001 the number of

Table 1. Numbers and percentages of people in the United States 65 years of age and over from 1900 to 1970, and as projected to 2030

Year	Number (millions)	Percentage of total population
1900	3.1	4.1
1940	9.0	6.8
1975	22.4	10.5
2000	31.8	11.7
2030	55.0	17.0

Table 2. Number and percentage of people in Britain 65 years of age and over from 1901 to 1971, and as projected to 2001

Year	Number (millions)	Percentage of total population
1901	1.5	4.0
1971	7.1	13.3
2001	10.8	18.5

elderly in the 75–79-year age group will increase by 19.8 percent, the 80–84-year group by 30.8 percent, and 85-and-over group by 46.3 percent. In the United States in 1900, the proportion of elderly who were 75 years and over was 29 percent, by 1970 it was 38 percent, and by the year 2000 it is expected that about 45 percent of the population 65 and over will be over 75 years of age (U.S. Bureau of the Census 1977). Because of this growth in the very old population in both countries, extra resources will be needed to cope with their health and social needs.

The elderly in both countries have relatively low incomes, and bare subsistence incomes often contribute to poor health. Although most of the elderly in Britain and the United States live healthy and active lives, a substantial number have some chronic illness, infirmity, or impairment that requires medical care. Chronic diseases such as heart disease and arthritis, as well as mental impairment and loss of sensory and motor abilities that frequently accompany old age and subsequently interfere with the ability of old people to live independently, contribute to the need for institutionalization for about 5 percent of the elderly in both countries. Presently, in both Britain and the United States, 95 percent of the elderly live in the community and 5 percent in some type of institutional facility (Office of Population Census and Survey 1974; United States Census Bureau 1973). It has been argued, however, that this 5 percent figure is deceptive, for it represents only the number of elderly in institutional facilities on any given day. Kastenbaum and Candy (1973) note that, whereas one in twenty elderly persons is in a nursing home on any given day, one in five will spend some time in a nursing home during his lifetime.

The elderly populations in Britain and the United States have many similarities. First, both countries have experienced a dramatic growth in the absolute as well as relative numbers of older people in the twentieth

Table 3. Current life expectancy for males and females in the United States and Britain

	Males	Females
United States	68.9	76.6
Britain	68.8	75.1

century. Second, due to high mortality rates for men in both countries, there is a predominance of women in the older population; consequently, elderly women are more likely to be living alone than elderly men. Third, the aged in both countries have relatively low incomes. And last, substantial numbers of elderly in Britain and the United States have some chronic illness that requires medical care.

Differences in the Approach to Geriatric Care

It is the attitude toward and the approach to the care of this 5 percent of the elderly, those in institutions, that this study addresses. Because the British geriatric service provides an excellent model of an innovative approach to long-term care, I felt that a cross-cultural comparative study would facilitate the identification of those criteria that contribute to quality care. Strictly speaking, one cannot compare an institution in Scotland, a small homogeneous country of five million people, with one in a country as large and culturally complex as the United States. For example, the homogeneity of the Scottish population and the heterogeneity of the population in the United States, and the difficulties encountered when comparing two such disparate populations, are obvious problems in such a comparison. Despite this shortcoming, however, I believe that the investigation of an institution within the unique structure of the British Geriatric Service will provide data from which we can learn and subsequently improve the quality of care for the institutionalized aged in the United States.

Britain's approach to the institutional care of the elderly has changed dramatically since World War II. First, beginning in the late 1940s, British physicians established geriatrics as a speciality. The subsequent development of the geriatric service has provided a unique structure for the assessment, rehabilitation, and provision for the continuing care of the aged in Britain; also, with the development of the geriatric service, geriatric care,

both acute and chronic, has become an integral part of the overall medical care structure. In the United States, by contrast, the majority of the
members of the American Geriatric Society are internists rather than geriatricians; and although acute care of the geriatric patient is a part of the
health care system, the care of the chronic, long-term, geriatric patient in
nursing homes is not within the mainstream of the medical care system.

Second, in Britain an attempt to keep the elderly person at home for as
long as possible has led to a heavy emphasis on the development of
supportive community services. But in the United States, supportive community services are poorly developed, and the phenomenal increase of
nursing home beds is dramatic evidence of the growing trend toward
institutionalizing of the elderly.

Third, much of the post-war legislation has been motivated by a desire
to treat all citizens equally; Britain has gradually abandoned the nine-
teenth-century philosophy that centered on a belief in custodial care as the
final answer (Townsend 1962:37).

Last, a major reason for selecting Scotland as the site for a comparative
study is the difference between the financing, organization, and delivery of
health care in Scotland and in the United States. In Britain a welfare state
has evolved, and within it the National Health Service (NHS) provides
medical care. The NHS, which came into being on 5 July 1948, pays for
virtually the entire range of health and medical care without regard to age,
income, need, or insurance qualification (see Chapter 7). By contrast, in
the United States the medical care system fits into our national concepts
of free enterprise and free choice coupled with individual responsibility.
The prototype for medical practice in the United States is the solo, private
entrepreneur charging a fee for services rendered. Public responsibility for
the financing of health care has been limited to groups such as members
of the armed forces, veterans, American Indians, the medically indigent,
and the elderly; health care in the United States remains largely a private,
fee-for-service system (Knowles 1977). Although Medicare and Medicaid
have provided considerable financial assistance for the elderly, those who
require long-term institutional care are required by the system to deplete
their personal finances before they are eligible for government aid. That is,
to qualify for Medicaid, the elderly must be indigent; they can have no
more than $1,500 in cash.

Hence, the progressive and innovative concept of British geriatric care,
which has developed under the auspices of the NHS, provides an interest-

ing model for comparison with long-term geriatric care in the United States.

Methodology

Using the anthropological field-work method, I drew the data in this study from three months of field work (July–September 1977) in a 96-bed, government-owned, long-term-care institution (Scottsdale) on the east coast of Scotland and four months of field work (January–April 1978) in a similar 85-bed proprietary institution (Pacific Manor) in a major Pacific Coast city in the United States.

In conducting the research, I used both participant observation and formal interviews to gather data. These two procedures are complementary in that interviewing allows for some standardization of data collection, whereas participant observation provides a more intimate view of social process and social interaction (Cicourel 1964:66). Participant observation, a technique associated with anthropological field work, is central to effective field work; hence, it is a major research tool used in anthropological research (Pelto 1970). Utilized as a scientific research tool, it involves the investigator in an active and intensive participation in the social or cultural context under study.

Participant observation was chosen as the primary research tool because I believe that direct observation of the elderly within the institution (their natural habitat), going about their daily activities in interaction with staff and others, can provide new insight into the problems of institutional care of the aged. Many survey-type institutional studies have looked at staffing patterns, staff attitudes, demographic characteristics, and the cost of care. However, other than Gubrium's (1975) study, which examines the social organization of care in one nursing home, there is to the best of my knowledge no other in-depth study of nursing homes. Additionally, a comparative study that combines intensive observation and interpretation of the dynamics of institutional life within the social-cultural context of each institution provides a unique contribution to anthropology and gerontology, and to health care professionals and policy makers in the field of aging. Therefore, I chose to study in depth one institution in each country rather than survey many in both countries. I acknowledge the limitations of such a study.

Selection of Institutions for Study

It was important to choose facilities that were comparable in the type of service provided. Geriatric institutions in the United States and Britain constitute a wide range of facilities, based on the type of care and the level of complexity of service provided, that includes extended-care facilities, skilled-nursing facilities, nursing homes, convalescent hospitals, homes for the aged, residential homes, sheltered housing, continuing or long-term-care units, psycho-geriatric units, and mental hospitals. This extensive, but not exhaustive, list of the various types of institutions that provide services to the elderly illustrates the need to limit one's study and also points out the potential difficulty in locating comparable institutions. For the purposes of this study, I chose to focus on institutions that provide medical services and nursing care to the elderly with chronic physical disabilities.[1]

Upon arriving in Scotland, I visited residential homes; sheltered housing; day-care hospitals; and geriatric assessment, rehabilitation, and continuing care units in three major cities. The continuing or long-term-care hospital was the facility most likely to be providing medical and nursing services to the disabled elderly, and in structure and provision of services it was most like the nursing home in the United States.

In the past, many reports and studies have focused on institutions that provide low-quality care. To fulfill the purpose of this study—the identification of institutional structures that contribute to high-quality care—I selected a model institution as a standard of excellence from which we could learn and subsequently improve the quality of care for the aged in the United States. Thus, although I describe conditions in a model institution, to be fair, it must be noted that not all institutions in Britain are of such a high caliber. In the past 30 years there has been an effort to raise the standards of care, and all of the facilities that I visited at random were fine indeed; yet there still exists a wide variation in the quality of institutional care.[2] For example, Halliburton and Wright (1973), in a study in

1. Although I am fully aware that the physically and mentally disabled who are institutionalized share many problems, I did not visit any psychogeriatric facilities or mental institutions for the elderly in either country. Hence, I will not compare my findings with previous studies on mental institutions.

2. See Chapter 7 for a description of some of the inadequacies still existent in British geriatric medicine that contribute to a variation in quality of care from one geriatric service to another.

England that included observation in fifty hospitals, found that, although the government has laid down certain minimum standards that must be met, a wide variation of services persists within the general framework. They conclude that although the institutionalized elderly were usually given security and affection (they found no evidence of cruelty) some of the elderly were treated in ways that denied them identity and dignity.

In selecting a nursing home for study in the United States, I looked for one similar to the Scottish institution in size, in the type of patient, and in the type of services provided to the elderly. In a comparative study, ownership of the facility would normally be a variable to hold constant. However, to select institutions most representative of each country, I had to forego this principle. In Britain the majority of the institutions for the elderly are government owned; thus a publicly owned facility was most representative. In the United States, by comparison, nursing homes, which house about 900,000 of the 1 million institutionalized elderly (Tiven 1971), are primarily proprietary or nonprofit, church-related homes.[3] About 80 percent of the institutions for the elderly and 96 percent of the nursing home beds are in proprietary homes (Abdellah 1976, Butler 1975:264); consequently, a commercially owned institution was selected for study. Proprietary homes may also have a high percentage of publicly supported or privately financed patients or some combination thereof. The proprietary nursing home with a high proportion of publicly supported persons is the most common type of nursing home in the United States (Gottesman 1974). And some investigators have found that the higher the percentage of welfare patients, the fewer the resources and the lower the quality of care. Conversely, proprietary homes with a high proportion of privately financed patients have more resources and provide a higher level of care (Kosberg and Tobin 1972; Gottesman 1974). Thus, whereas the proprietary publicly funded institution is the most representative, I did not want to compare the best of Scotland with the worst possible analogue in the United States. I selected for study, therefore, a proprietary home (reputed to be one of the finest in the city) that would admit only privately funded patients.

3. Some of the nonprofit, church-related homes, such as the Jewish Homes for the Aged, are known to provide excellent care. It must be noted, however, that such institutions provide care to only about 10–14 percent of the elderly and that they serve the more socially advantaged elderly. These homes have a high proportion of private-pay patients, and the residents are more likely to have children and others in the community who are actively interested in their care (Gottesman 1974).

These two institutions obviously are not typical of all such settings in the two countries, yet I believe they provide a representative illustration of institutionalized geriatric care in Britain and the United States. I shall illustrate, moreover, how these institutions are an integral part of the broader structures in each society that have to do with institutional care; an intensive study of two facilities will provide a more general picture of generic problems and possible solutions than would otherwise be possible.

2

The Institutional
Setting

For purposes of health care delivery, Scotland is divided into fifteen regions, each of which is further subdivided into districts (Kane and Kane 1976). Upon arrival in Scotland, I visited geriatric services in three of these regions and decided that an east coast city of 230,000, which I shall call Dunhaven, was best suited to my research goals. My decision to study an institution in Dunhaven was in large measure influenced by the hospitable reception I received from the chief geriatrician in this region. He assured me access to any medical records I wished to see, and he gave permission to observe and visit patients on all hospital wards and in all institutions attached to the geriatric service. He introduced me to key personnel in nursing, medicine, and supportive services (such as occupational therapy, physiotherapy, and social services) and invited me to attend conferences with medical house officers and nursing staffs. Further, he suggested that I accompany him on ward rounds and domiciliary visits. Finally, he informed me that within the geriatric service there was a "model" 96-bed long-term-care hospital. This institution (Scottsdale) proved to be an ideal facility for an intensive study of long-term care, and it was there that I did the majority of my work.

The geriatric service in Dunhaven, established in 1955, is an integral part of a large general hospital that is associated with a university medical center. Approximately 150 of the 650 beds of this geriatric service are located physically in a general hospital. These beds are used for assess-

13

ment and rehabilitation; simultaneously they permit both medical and nursing students to receive experience in geriatric problems as part of their clinical training in general medicine. Half of the remaining 500 beds, all of which are used for long-term care, are in hospitals in or near the major city in the region; the others are located in small hospitals in six outlying communities. As mentioned earlier, an effort is made by personnel to use the term "continuing care units"; however, in practice the terms "long-stay units," "long-term units," and "continuing care units" are used interchangeably both in the literature and in speaking. These terms refer to those units or beds utilized by the chronically ill (most of whom are aged) who require long-term health care in an institutional setting.

How the Geriatric Service Functions

Three geriatric consultants (or "geriatricians"), all specialists in geriatric medicine, a senior registrar (a physician in the final stage of specialist training that leads to a consultant post), and other junior medical staff members provide the medical care for the geriatric service in this region. The consultants receive approximately thirteen hundred referrals a year from other hospital specialists and from general practitioners throughout the region. Following the request for referral, the patient is visited either in his home or, if he is already an in-patient, in the hospital to assess both the medical problem and the social situation. Each consultant makes about three hundred domiciliary visits a year. Since there is a shortage of beds for geriatric patients, the home assessment facilitates the geriatrician's setting of priorities for admission to the assessment unit. It is also advantageous for patients since they are seen very quickly, usually on the day the referral request is made. Moreover, the home-assessment visit prevents an unnecessary hospital admission that can be traumatic for the elderly; and the home visit provides an excellent opportunity for the geriatrician to establish rapport with a new patient.

If the patient requires hospitalization, he is admitted to the assessment and rehabilitation unit. In some Scottish geriatric services, these are distinct and separate units; but in the Dunhaven region, they are one and the same. The geriatricians emphasize that many elderly patients suffer from multiple disorders that may require extensive diagnostic procedures as well as the services of a specialist in geriatric medicine. They believe it essential that the assessment and rehabilitation unit be located within a major hospital that provides all the necessary diagnostic and rehabilitation services.

Following diagnosis, treatment and rehabilitation become the focus of care. In rehabilitating an elderly patient, the aim is to achieve the maximum possible degree of independence in self-care. Geriatric rehabilitation is a complex group effort involving nurses; doctors; social workers; physiotherapists; chiropodists; occupational, speech, and diversional therapists; and voluntary workers and visitors. Each member has an important role in the rehabilitation of the patient: successful rehabilitation requires close communication and cooperation between all.

Since many elderly patients suffer from such problems as arthritis, fractures, and cerebrovascular accidents with resulting hemiplegia, a primary function of the physiotherapist is to assess the patient's condition and help him become mobile and independent. Occupational therapy is closely aligned to physiotherapy. The occupational therapist provides and supervises exercises for specific disabilities, such as crafts and games that exercise hand and finger joints. The occupational therapy department also has innumerable items designed to keep an elderly person as independent as possible, both in the hospital and upon return home. For example, following a cerebrovascular accident that paralyzes a side, an elderly person may have difficulty eating. Thus, a plate guard attached to the rim of the plate will enable the person who has the use of only one hand to eat without pushing food off the plate. There are also forks and spoons with a specific slant designed for patients who cannot rotate their wrists, and other eating utensils with large, thick handles for easier grasping by those who can no longer completely close their hands.

The occupational therapy department also has a small simulated household unit where the therapist can assess the degree of functional disability of aged patients prior to their discharge. Here a patient is observed cooking a meal, dressing, using bathroom facilities, and getting in and out of bed. Some people, for instance, may be able to get into bed without assistance, but perhaps due to arthritis they cannot pull up the covers. Special provision must be made for such people in their homes. Following assessment, the therapist recommends the aids and devices necessary in the home if the patient is to be resettled in the community.

Occupational therapy and physiotherapy treat and rehabilitate the body; equally important is the diversional therapy that treats the mind. A diversional therapist attempts to find meaningful projects to stimulate a patient mentally and provide some activity of functional value. In diversional therapy, for example, patients make trays, children's toys, knitwear, and other items that are purchased by hospital employees. Finally, the social worker fulfills an important function in working as a liaison between staff and relatives in planning for a patient's future, whether at home or in another institution.

The assessment and rehabilitation unit at Dunhaven admits about one thousand patients a year. Approximately one-half are treated and then discharged to their own homes, to sheltered housing, or to a residential facility. Another quarter die in the hospital, and the final quarter are transferred to a continuing care unit like Scottsdale.

Scottsdale

Many of the institutional facilities in Scotland are very old, and Scottsdale is no exception. A brief history of the facility is in order because the feelings and attitudes toward admission to it today are in part governed by the original intention for which the hospital was founded. Scottsdale was founded in 1857 as a hospital for the "deserving poor," to provide moderate comfort for local persons who, because of incurable illness, could not earn a living. Originally it housed only six patients. Since, by definition, these patients were "deserving," no stigma was attached to their status. This distinction was important at a time when many cities were building poorhouses, when an acceptance of this kind of help carried the stigma of a semi-criminal act (Gilbert 1966:14). Actually, from the outset Scottsdale had a snobbish appeal, and it quickly developed a reputation for being an excellent hospital: today it receives generous endowments that provide amenities for its long-term patients.

As the number of patients requiring long-term care increased over the years, the hospital expanded. In 1882 the present site was purchased and 2 years later a new hospital opened with accommodations for fifty-five patients. In 1891 an additional wing was added, and 10 years later a large recreation hall was built. With the introduction of the National Health Service in 1948, Scottsdale became a government continuing care geriatric hospital. By then its facilities were inadequate, and in 1967 it was completely rehabilitated and a new, 26-bed wing was added. The number of beds in the old wards was reduced simultaneously to make the environment more pleasant and spacious. Today Scottsdale accommodates ninety-six chronically ill patients, most of whom are over 65 years of age. Surrounded by beautiful gardens, it is situated in a fine residential area on a hill with a grand view of the city and the sea. In summer the gardens supply fresh flowers for the patient wards, and a greenhouse on the grounds provides plants and flowers for the hospital rooms during the long, dark, winter months. Each Friday the gardeners—there are six—cut a variety of flowers and one of the hospital maids makes bouquets to be placed in various locations throughout the hospital.

The hospital is a sturdy, gray, granite, two-story structure divided into four units: one of 18 beds for male patients, and three of 25, 26, 27 beds, respectively, for female patients. Within these four units, there are ten private rooms, one semi-private room and the remaining patient accommodations are in 3-, 4-, and 6-bed wards. The rooms and wards are typical of hospitals, but although parts of the hospital are nearly 100 years old, all hallways and rooms are decorated in pleasant pastel colors. There are large windows in every room and even on rainy days, of which there are many, the inside atmosphere of the hospital is not depressing and dreary, but rather bright and cheerful. The large windows also provide the patients with lovely views of the gardens, the city, and the sea.

The recreation hall is used for the weekly church service, and on rainy days, when patients cannot go out of doors, many gather there for morning coffee. Although this wood-panelled room is large, it is very warm and cozy. Beautiful antique pieces of copper grace the hearth and mantel of the fireplace, and lovely oil paintings hang on the walls. There is a fine organ in the room, some antique pieces of furniture, and always a large bouquet of fresh flowers. The hall has the appearance and ambience that one might find in a private Scottish home rather than in a hospital.

The new wing includes two sun porches on the second floor and a large sunroom on the first floor. These rooms are also warm, cheerful and conducive to interaction among small groups. Another attractive feature of the hospital is a small shop operated by one of the patients; here staff members and patients come daily to purchase snack food, toiletries, and other items for their own use or as gifts for others.

Scottsdale's facilities and surrounding gardens provide patients with a choice of where and how they can spend their day. For those confined to wheelchairs but who still have the use of their upper extremities, ramps on each level provide access to the verandah and the grounds. For example, Mrs. Milne, a 95-year-old woman with a fractured hip, wheels herself out on the verandah nearly every day; for her it is essential to go outdoors daily for fresh air. She is an independent woman, and despite the admonishment of the staff, can be found on the verandah even on cold days. "Others think it is too cold," she observed, "but I go out to keep myself going." On warm sunny days, dozens of patients are sitting on the verandah, neatly dressed and protected from the sun by wide-brimmed straw hats. Other groups of patients are reading books and visiting with one another over morning coffee in the lounges or sunrooms.

Although few patients ever leave Scottsdale—"This is a hospital for life," said one patient—it is not a depressing or morbid institution. On the contrary, patient morale seems very high. The matron of the hospital explained that staff do not dwell upon the fact that patients will be there for the rest of their lives: "We try to make it as homely as possible, and we have as few restrictions as possible. I think life is sweet to them, whatever the quality, and they do not dwell on death." Staff do not shy away from the subject of death, however; they allow patients to express their feelings. Recently one woman said, "All of my friends are away, and I am ready to go anytime."

Each morning as I entered the hospital, traditional Scottish or modern music flowed into the hallways from record players situated in each ward. There were television sets in every ward and most private rooms, gifts from the "Friends of Scottsdale" (a volunteer group), but they were usually not turned on until midafternoon and evening.

The maids hurried about the hallways, humming softly as they went about their work. Other staff, neatly groomed, all in their respective and appropriate uniforms, industriously performed their duties. There was a sense of order, organization, and purpose to their work; there was also a strong sense of everyone working together. According to one of the kitchen staff, "We are one big family here, and we all work together; everyone is friendly to one another."

Pacific Manor

At Scottsdale all of the patients had been admitted following extensive treatment and rehabilitation in the assessment and rehabilitation unit of the geriatric service. However, in the United States, unlike in Scotland, geriatric medicine is not a specialty; there is no equivalent to the geriatric service for providing medical care for the elderly. As a result the majority of the elderly in the United States are cared for by private physicians, and the 5 percent who need institutional care are admitted to nursing homes either directly from their own homes or from acute-care hospitals. Although some reports indicate 50–55 percent of patients come to long-term-care facilities from their own or relatives' homes (e.g., Special Committee on Aging: U.S. Senate 1974), at Pacific Manor only 6 percent came directly from their own or a relative's home. The majority—85 percent— were admitted to the nursing home directly from an acute-care hospital, 6 percent were admitted from their home, and 9 percent came from other nursing homes or "board and care" homes (which provide residential care only). Although it is widely believed that many elderly patients were admitted to nursing homes from state mental hospitals during the deinstitutionalization of the late 1960s and early 1970s, only one such patient had been admitted to Pacific Manor.[1]

Pacific Manor is located in an area of the city that is partly commercial and partly residential. It is a high crime area. During my first visit I was carefully warned by the director of nursing services not to visit the facility after 6 P.M., not to carry a purse, and not to leave anything of value locked in my car. If I had to leave after dark, she cautioned, one of the staff should accompany me to my car. At 7 P.M. an orderly places heavy chains with locks on the doors of the institution "to keep the good guys in and the bad guys out."

The building, constructed in 1966, is divided into two units of 40–45 beds each (Unit A and Unit B) and is well planned for elderly, often disabled, people. Rooms are designed to accommodate two patients, with a bathroom (a toilet and washbasin) between each pair of rooms. Each patient has a small closet and one drawer for personal belongings. Although rooms are "efficient," they are relatively small and crowded; wheelchair patients have difficulty in moving about in them. And the sliding wooden doors on the closets often come off the track or stick in a half-open position, making it difficult for patients to reach their personal belongings. Some of these problems are avoided, of course, by the few

---

1. For further information on deinstitutionalization and decarceration see: Ellen L. Bassuk and Samuel Gerson, "Deinstitutionalization and Mental Health Services, *Scientific American* 238:2, February 1978, pp. 46–53; Wilma A. Donahue, "What About Our Responsibility Toward the Abandoned Elderly?" *The Gerontologist* 18:2, April 1978, pp. 102–11; and Andrew T. Scull, *Decarceration, Community Treatment and the Deviant: A Radical View,* Englewood Cliffs: Prentice-Hall, 1977.

patients willing and able to pay for single accommodations; one bed is removed from a standard room, leaving ample space. At the time of the study, only three patients were so accommodated.

All bedrooms and lounges are on the main floor of the building, an arrangement that enables both ambulatory and wheelchair patients to move about freely. Bedrooms that face the patio, with its flowering plants, are very pleasant; those that face the front street or the rear alley are less so (see accompanying figure for the floor plan of Pacific Manor).[2]

It is noteworthy that although all patients, those who can walk and those confined to wheelchairs, have easy access to the patio few make use of this very pleasant area. Even on warm, sunny days there are never more than three or four patients in the courtyard. One patient, Mrs. Levine, is on the patio every afternoon: "I would go crazy if I had to stay in my room all day." She does not understand why other patients do not join her on the patio. Few ever do.

Even with the hallways carpeted in bright red, the potential feeling of warmth is lost because they are easily soiled and require frequent cleaning. Often from morning until late afternoon hallways are being vacuumed, and the resulting high noise level is disturbing to patients, staff, and visitors alike.

The lounges are the center of activity, and many patients are placed there early in the morning, to remain for the major part of the day. Sofas and chairs line the walls; long tables with plastic tablecloths occupy the center of the room. One of the two lounges has a large color television set, nearly always on. In the other a piano stands in the corner. Color posters and black-and-white photographs of patients, taken on an outdoor excursion the preceding summer, are tacked on the walls. A few old books and some outdated magazines on the bookshelves provide the only reading material for patients. The room is well lighted and sunny, but it is not really pleasant or cheerful. Nor is it tastefully decorated; instead, it appears cluttered and untidy, and there are none of the small comforts or conveniences that one would normally find in a home. On rare occasions a bouquet of fresh flowers, donated to the nursing home, is placed in the lounge or in the front foyer. Each day twenty to twenty-five patients sit in each of the two lounges; however, some refuse to go to the day rooms

2. It would have been desirable to include a floor plan of Scottsdale. Because of multiple additions to the building, however, the architectural structure is complex and such a plan would have been difficult to prepare.

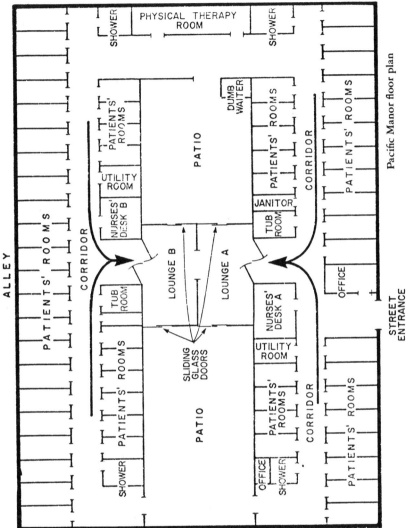

Pacific Manor floor plan

because of the strong odor of urine and because they find the rooms noisy and unpleasant. "Some days they force me to go in there," complained Mrs. Peterson, "but I would rather stay here alone in my room." Mrs. Levine added, "I went in there for one of the activities last week, but I told them I am never going back again. Some of the patients urinated right on the floor during the entertainment."

Thus, although Pacific Manor is modern and conveniently planned, and although it offers a potentially excellent physical environment for the disabled elderly, it does not compare favorably with the older, less efficient Scottish institution.

3

Life in the
Institution

Having looked at the physical environment at Scottsdale and Pacific Manor, we turn in this chapter to a view of the routine of daily life in the two institutions. Mealtime, social, recreational, and work projects; the provision of personal care; and visitors provide the major daily activities for the institutionalized aged.

Food

Food is an important aspect of care in institutional life. Beyond providing nutrients for life, it has religious and symbolic significance and is a social and recreational activity (Whiteman 1966). For those who must spend the last days of their lives restricted to an institution, mealtime is an important event, and good food can contribute greatly to patients' satisfaction and their quality of life.

A part of this study was designed to provide quantitative and qualitative data to measure patients' evaluation of their care. To obtain some idea of the range of opinion, I asked 25 percent of the patients in each institution a set of structured questions. Responses to the questions were ranked on a scale of 1 to 5, 1 representing complete dissatisfaction with care and 5 representing complete satisfaction with care. Subsequently, a mean was computed.

23

Patients' Evaluation of Food at Scottsdale

Patients in each institution were asked "How is the food here?" At Scottsdale the responses were overwhelmingly positive; 100 percent of those interviewed expressed complete or nearly complete satisfaction with the food: the mean response was 4.8. Patients commented on the quality, the frequency of food service, and the pleasure derived in selecting from a menu.

The quality of the food at Scottsdale was considered very high by patients; some said they would not eat so well were they living at home. In fact, the hospital had gained such a fine reputation for its food that health personnel frequently came to Scottsdale for meals before going on duty at neighboring hospitals. A sampling of the patients' responses about the quality of food is indicative of their satisfaction:

> "The food here is very good—anyone who complains about it is not accustomed to good food. I have never heard anyone complain about it."

> "It is very good, very good indeed; nothing to complain about at all."

> "The food here is very lovely—very good soups—we get delicious scotch broth that is jolly good."

The patients at Scottsdale were also satisfied with the amount of food served; they received three meals a day plus nourishment between meals and at bedtime. One patient confided, "The food is very good; we get far too much." Breakfast was served at 7 A.M., tea and biscuits at 10 A.M. and 2 P.M., lunch (a three-course meal) at 12:30 P.M., high tea (a small, hot meal) at 5 P.M. and a hot drink or fruit juice at 7 P.M.

Although the quality and quantity were important, the selective menu was the outstanding feature of meals at Scottsdale. Patients were given a choice of three entrées and three desserts for their midday and evening meal. The pleasure this choice affords crept into most discussions of food:

> "The food is very good; we get three choices for lunch and three choices for tea."

> "I think the food is very good, and we get a menu. The nurses

come every day, and we can choose from three items for the main course and dessert."

One patient who had been at the hospital for 40 years elaborated:

> "The food here is good, very good; we get everything, roast pork, roast lamb, a good breakfast—not a cooked breakfast—they don't have time for that. But we get cereal, rolls, and sometimes on Sundays we get jam tarts and nice scones. There is good variety in the food and we get a choice of entrée."

Despite the high quality and ample choice of food, patients at Scottsdale make frequent trips to the shop within the hospital to purchase sweets (biscuits, cookies, and cakes) for their morning and afternoon tea. Having personal money and a shop within the hospital provides them yet another option and some freedom in their choice of food.

Food was attractively served at Scottsdale. Small tables were decorated with flowers and set with cloth placemats and napkins. Most patients ate in small, congenial groups on the sunporches or in the wards, while others chose to eat alone in their rooms. Food was a source of enjoyment; mealtime, a pleasant, social experience.

Patients' Evaluation of Food at Pacific Manor

By contrast, at Pacific Manor food was often a source of displeasure. Of those interviewed, 40 percent said the food was very poor, 45 percent were moderately satisfied, while only 15 percent were very satisfied with the food; the mean response was 2.5. Those who indicated satisfaction with the food were neutral rather than very positive. Some patients said, for example, "The food is good," "I get enough to eat," and "It is all right." Another had mixed feelings: "The food is all right, but I have no teeth and I have to eat with a spoon; I have no teeth!" Patients who were dissatisfied with the food complained about its poor quality, the lack of choice, inadequate amounts, the absence of fresh fruits and vegetables, tough meat, and the unpleasant environment at mealtime. The evening meal was considered especially poor.

Although more than half the patients interviewed were moderately to very satisfied with the food, those who were dissatisfied expressed appreciable anger. Eighty-year-old Mrs. Tyler complained, "The food is just terrible; if I didn't have the cookies and graham crackers that my sister brings me, I would starve." Mrs. Tyler's normal weight is 100–105 pounds; she has been losing weight recently and now weighs 83 pounds, a loss she blames on poor food. Other comments about the food at Pacific Manor detail its shortcomings:

> "I don't like the food; I guess it is good enough, but we only get salads once in a while and there is never any choice of food."

> "We almost never get desserts; we have pie at Thanksgiving and Christmas, and sometimes we have cake, but it is like straw."

> "We used to have regular ice cream once in a while, but now they put in one of those ice cream machines, probably because it is cheaper, but it doesn't taste like ice cream."

A few patients have relatives and friends who bring food to supplement their diet, but because of the danger of theft, patients cannot keep food in kitchen refrigerators. Mrs. Levine is one who has first-hand experience: "The food here is just terrible; I would starve to death if my family did not bring me food. . . . I can never eat the evening meal; it is much worse than lunch." Her family and friends bring her fruit, cheese, and pastry; however, unless she keeps them hidden in her room, they are stolen. Initially, she put the food in the refrigerator, only to find it gone at mealtime. On one occasion she included a note that pleaded, "Please don't take this fruit; it is all I have and I have no way of getting out to get any." Yet on the next day the fruit had disappeared.

Mrs. Levine also explained how difficult she finds it to eat her meals in the lounge, with its prevailing odor of urine. Nonambulatory patients are placed in the lounge after breakfast, and most remain there throughout the day. Incontinent patients sometimes urinate during mealtime. Others with urine-soaked clothes remain in the dining area. The staff make no attempt to control the problem by taking patients to the bathroom before meals or by changing soiled clothing before mealtime.

As mentioned above, in addition to its nutritional value, food has other functions; it has symbolic significance, and offering food to someone conveys an expression of caring for that person. While I was visiting with Mr. Fuller one day, he began to cry as he talked of his wife; she had died a week earlier. I tried to comfort him and after the crying stopped asked if he might like some fruit juice. "Yes," he replied. I went to the nurse in charge, explained the situation, and asked if I might take him some juice. "No," she answered, "the juice is only for the diabetic patients." It seemed incredible that anyone could deny a recently bereaved man a glass of juice. I walked to the other unit, where the nurse in charge gave me a glass of grape juice. Mr. Fuller drank some of the juice and then poured in some water. "It tastes like champagne," he smiled. "I want to stretch it a bit."

The experience of eating at Pacific Manor, then, does not compare favorably with that at Scottsdale. The Scottish patients were 100 percent pleased with the quality and quantity of food and thoroughly enjoyed having a choice of menu. But at Pacific Manor many patients were unhappy with the quality and quantity of food and objected to the lack of choice. Although no systematic information about the adequacy of diets was obtained at Pacific Manor, the comments of the patients suggest that this is an area for inquiry. At Scottsdale, it is clear, mealtime is a pleasant social experience; whereas at Pacific Manor, it is a socially and esthetically unpleasant experience.

Social, Recreational, and Work Activities

It is important to recognize that long-term-care facilities are "homes" for disabled, elderly people; thus, attention to social, recreational, and meaningful work activities is essential. In order for the institutionalized person to be integrated socially and enjoy a meaningful life, it is desirable to create an environment within the institution that approximates that of an older person in the outside world.

Activities at Scottsdale

At Scottsdale patients are provided with regular, planned activities, and they are also enabled and encouraged to pursue individual interests. There is a weekly Sunday morning church service, a full-length film (selected by a patient committee) every Thursday, and on Fridays a gathering in the recreational hall, where an organist plays their favorite songs.

Diversional therapy and reading are the favorite activities of patients at Scottsdale. On Tuesdays and Fridays a diversional therapist is on duty to assist them in making articles that can be sold or given to others as gifts. Patients make beautiful trays and toys for children; they knit, crochet, and do needlework. These activities are highly valued: 60 percent of the patients interviewed said making articles in therapy was their favorite activity. "I wouldn't want to live if I weren't useful," remarked one woman. Forty percent of the patients interviewed cited reading as a favorite activity. Fortunately, the hospital has a voluminous library with a wide selection of literary works as well as books with large print for those with poor vision. Every two weeks volunteers visit each unit, and patients may select as many books as they wish from the library cart.

Receiving visitors and making outings were singled out as highly valued social activities. The hospital has no limitation on visiting hours— family and friends (with children) are welcome at all times. Relatives are also encouraged to take out the elderly for an evening, a day, or the weekend. Eighty percent of the patients interviewed have relatives or friends who take them home or for an outing several times during the year. Arrangements for pleasure trips are also made for those who have no relatives. The Social Service Department in Dunhaven and the Multiple Sclerosis Society have minibuses that accommodate four wheelchair patients; therefore, most patients can make short excursions to a park or a nearby castle, take a ride in the country, or have dinner in a local restaurant.

Two outstanding features of the Scottish institution are the "Friends of Scottsdale" and the "Scottsdale Social Club." The former is a volunteer group that provides money for the purchase of luxury items for the aged. This old and distinguished organization originated with a small group of people who initially gave a half-crown each (about $0.25) to establish a charitable fund at Scottsdale. From this meager beginning, the fund has grown into a considerable sum that now provides residents with virtually anything that will add to their comfort and pleasure. "The patients want for nothing," beamed one sister (the equivalent term for charge nurse): "The 'Friends' buy them anything they want." They have purchased the color television sets, music equipment, and records for each ward; and annually they buy birthday and Christmas gifts for each resident. Periodically, gifts of luxury food items such as melons, strawberries, and salmon are provided for the patients. "The Friends" also make funds available for "taxi runs" for those who have no family. For example, a patient may take a taxi to visit a friend, go shopping, or take a drive around the city. There is one man at Scottsdale whose only friend is blind. Every month "The Friends" pay his taxi fare to the hospital so that he can visit his old companion.

The "Scottsdale Social Club" was founded by the house physician, who felt an evening social once a month would be of value to the patients. Officers for the club are elected from the personnel and residents of the hospital. The Club "gives them something to look forward to," explained the matron, "and something to talk about with family and friends." The social club meets on the first Wednesday of each month for an evening's entertainment, followed by refreshments of sausage rolls, cake, and tea. The patients, dressed in their finest clothing, attend a program planned in keeping with seasonal and national holidays. In December, for example, there is a Christmas party; in the summer a garden party; and in February, when all the people of Scotland celebrate the birthday of the Scottish bard, Robert Burns, there is a "Robbie Burns supper" with "haggis, tatties, and neeps" (a traditional meat dish, potatoes, and turnips), followed by a reading of Burns's poetry. The patients thoroughly enjoy these social evenings, which help to keep them a part of the Scottish social and cultural life. These are also occasions when staff and patients mix socially. Staff at all levels (the house physician, matron, nurses, and auxiliary workers) attend the social, help with the entertainment, and serve the food; this helps establish social bonds between the staff and patients.

Activities at Pacific Manor

Pacific Manor employs an activity director; she plans a weekly program for the patients and posts a monthly calendar with an activity scheduled for each day. Activities include bingo on Mondays and Wednesdays, table games (checkers and dominoes), musical entertainment, a short film biweekly, and church services for all denominations at various times throughout the week. Despite the many planned activities, when patients were asked "What do you like most?" 50 percent gave responses that indicated their boredom—"I just lay here"; "I haven't been doing very much; I don't do much of anything but walk around, and I hardly do anything"—25 percent said they liked to read, 20 percent liked the musical programs, and 5 percent answered that they watch television once in a while. One woman remarked, "I watch TV just to get out of my room."

Pacific Manor's activities are clearly of a lower quality than those at Scottsdale: patients are not involved in the planning; there is no outdoor recreation and no meaningful work. Because of the lack of significant work, days are filled with meaningless activity; and this must account, at least in part, for the boredom mentioned above. Those functions that are planned, although numerous, are often of poor quality.

It is the quality and not the quantity of activity that is important to the institutionalized aged. If social activities are of poor quality, not only are they boring, but they are also demeaning For instance, many do not like bingo, but those who do are denied some pleasure in the game because the prizes they win have no value. When a patient wins a game of bingo, he or she may choose a prize from a large cardboard box that contains such items as an old comb, motel-size bars of soap, an old shoe horn, and cast-off costume jewelry. "The prizes aren't worth anything," Mrs. Tyler observed, "but I play just to have something to do." The activity director offered a pragmatic explanation: "I figure they are not paying anything to play, so why should we buy prizes for them?"

Both institutions have weekly films for the patients, but again, there is a difference in quality. At Scottsdale regular, full-length films are rented; *The Sound of Music* and *The Other Side of the Mountain* were selected by the patients, and many commented on how they enjoyed these films. At Pacific Manor there is no money to rent films. "I virtually have no budget," said the activity director, "so I get films wherever I can get them without cost." One source of free films is a children's day camp; thus, many of the films are actually meant for children. "I don't go to the films," one woman mentioned, "they're rather childish and amateur."

The religious services provide another illustration of the difference in the quality of planned activities. The service at Scottsdale is performed regularly every Sunday at 9:30 A.M. Patients dress in their "Sunday best," enjoy organ music and use hymnals, and participate actively. Following the service, coffee and biscuits are served and the minister visits with the residents. It is a solemn, dignified service closely parallel to a Presbyterian church service I attended in the community. Conversely, at Pacific Manor patients are not dressed properly for church—some attend in their robes and slippers—an untuned piano provides the music, and throughout the service there is a steady stream of traffic through the lounge where the worship is held. Staff and visitors, rather than walking around the hallway to get from one unit to another, pass directly through the lounge during

the ceremony. The church service at Pacific Manor clearly
semble what one would find in the community; indeed, it
fertile imagination to think that one was in a bona fide rel¡

At both institutions several patients said they did not
activities and would prefer to sit in their room to read, sew, or crochet.
Whereas at Scottsdale many patients are engaged in these individual activities, at Pacific Manor only one woman has been observed doing nee-
dlepoint. There is no library, occupational therapy, or diversional therapy
at Pacific Manor; nor is there a provision for books, current magazines, or
materials for creative work. Many residents sit idle or aimlessly pace the
hallways.

The lack of outdoor activity is unbelievable and unhealthy; the majority of patients never get sunshine or outdoor exercise. There are no
grounds surrounding the building, and because Pacific Manor is located
in a high crime area, walking on the nearby streets would be unsafe.
However, despite these unmanageable problems, even the "safe" patio is
used by only two or three patients. This lack of use is incredible in that 54
percent are mobile (37 percent can walk unaided and 17 percent with
help). Patients seem to have developed a fear of going outside. "I could
go with someone," said Mrs. Tyler, "but I am afraid to go out on the
patio." "I go to the window and to the door and look out," added another woman, "but I wouldn't go out alone." Despite their fears, some
want to go out and recognize the importance of getting out: "I never go
out," explained Mrs. Soreno, "I think we get stupid when we stay in, but I
can't ask my niece or the nurses to take me."

Although many patients at Scottsdale are taken for excursions by family, friends, and volunteer groups, at Pacific Manor few ever leave the
facility—75 percent said they never get out of the nursing home for short
trips, 15 percent had been out on one occasion, and 10 percent have
family who take them out on a regular basis. There is one planned outing
during the year: a local radio station provides a bus and twenty-five to
thirty patients are driven to the country for a picnic. The lack of opportunity for outings seems to result in a lack of interest and an increased
fear of going out. Mrs. Sullivan has been at Pacific Manor for 9 years, yet
she has been out on only one occasion. "I guess after a while you don't
miss it," she remarked. Her one excursion was a trip, 3 years ago, to the
downtown office of an ophthalmologist. She took a taxi and was terrified
of the traffic: "I closed my eyes during the entire trip." Because patients

do not get out, they become isolated within the institution and lose contact with the real world.

Provision of Personal Care

In many long-term-care facilities in the United States, there is little emphasis on diagnosis, treatment, and rehabilitation; the focus of care is custodial, and the daily routine revolves around getting patients up in the morning, bathing them, and overseeing visiting hours.

Bathing and Grooming at Scottsdale

The patients at Scottsdale prefer tub baths to showers; therefore, despite the difficulty involved in putting them into the tub (there are no orderlies and 94 percent of the patients are either partially or totally immobile), baths are given once weekly (a weekly bath is quite normal by Scottish standards). A mechanical lifting apparatus transfers heavy patients into the tub. There is no fixed schedule for baths; the nursing staff give baths at their convenience and keep a record of when they are given. In addition to weekly baths, patients receive basins of water in the morning and afternoon for washing their hands and face before meals. And each time the bedpan is used, the patient's back and perineal area are washed, dried, and rubbed with lotion. If it is not "bath day," after their breakfast patients are helped out of bed, dressed, and placed in an area of their choosing. At 10 A.M., nurse aides serve coffee and biscuits to them wherever they are—on the verandah, the sunporch, or in their rooms.

Patients at Scottsdale wear fashionable personal clothing, jewelry, and makeup; they take a keen interest in their personal appearance. "I get shaved every day and have a haircut every fortnight," Mr. Simpson offered with some pleasure; "I like to be tidy." Barbers and hair dressers come to the hospital regularly. All female patients have their hair done biweekly by the hair dresser, and in between, if necessary, the nurses wash and set their hair. "The hair dresser takes special care to style each person's hair to suit their personality," explained the matron. There is individuality in their dress and appearance, and they look neat and well groomed at all times.

Bathing and Grooming at Pacific Manor

Pacific Manor patients are bathed three times a week, in theory, at least. Those in the "A" beds (the bed near the door) are bathed on Monday,

Wednesday, and Friday; those in the "B" beds (the bed near the window), on Tuesday, Thursday, and Saturday. In practice, however, this schedule is not always followed. The nurse aides and orderlies feel they are over-worked, so they decide who will be bathed. "I'll be frank with you," one of the aides confided, "I didn't give all of my baths this morning; I just have too much to do." Each worker has seven to eight patients, half of whom should be bathed each day. The nurse in charge of this unit is totally unaware of and unconcerned about what is taking place at the patient-care level.

On days when patients are not bathed, the staff are expected to provide basins of water for them to wash their hands and face. "They are sup-posed to wash our hands and face every morning," said Mrs. Levine; "I get my care because I know what is happening, but my roommate doesn't know what is going on and more often than not they don't give her any morning care."

The bathing procedure at Pacific Manor contrasts markedly with that at Scottsdale. At first glance and in a quantitative way, one might con-clude that three baths a week is superior to a weekly bath; however, a description of the bathing procedure at Pacific Manor will illustrate that such is not the case. Patients who are to be bathed are taken out of bed and placed on "shower chairs," upon which they must wait, sometimes for hours, before being taken to the shower room. The "shower chair" is a metal chair on rollers, but in place of a regular seat, it has a toilet seat. Many patients cannot distinguish this chair from a toilet. "Whenever they put my roommate on the shower chair, she urinates on the floor," Mrs. Levine observed. Many patients also have bowel movements while wait-ing on this chair; of course, the unpleasant sight and odor of urine and feces is nearly inescapable.

Little attention is given to patient modesty at bathtime; while waiting for a shower, patients are clothed only in short hospital gowns, and men and women are bathed simultaneously in the same shower room. "It's disgusting," complained Mrs. Peterson, "but what can we do?" Most pa-tients accept this violation of their modesty and dignity in silence, as this example illustrates: Mr. Daniels is a very proud and dignified 93-year-old man; he had been the president of a large clothing industry. His daughter visits daily, takes home his laundry, and keeps an ample supply of clothing available. "He has always been meticulous about his dress," she remarked. I was horrified one morning therefore to see an orderly pulling Mr. Daniels backwards—sitting in a shower chair and clad only in an undershirt—down the hallway. The orderly placed him in the shower room and said, "Now you stay there." Immediately to Mr. Daniels' right an aide was giving a shower to a female patient. Some patients, because they are scantily dressed, get cold while waiting for their shower, and others describe the shower as an ordeal. "The water is always cold," snapped Mr. Gray. The many negative circumstances associated with bathing make it an unpleasant rather than a pleasant experience.

In contrast to their Scottish counterparts, many of the patients at Pacific Manor are not well groomed and neatly dressed. The men are shaved only every three to four days; consequently, many have a heavy growth of beard. Mr. Daniels's daughter found this particularly troubling: "I am embarrassed to have his friends visit. He shaved every day of his life when he was at home." A hairdresser comes to the nursing home weekly, she charges $6.00 for a shampoo and set and $22.50 for a permanent. Since half of the patients are on Medicaid, these prices are obviously not within their means; thus, many women do not have attractive hairstyles. Patients' clothing is frequently soiled and in need of repair. Several remarked that their personal clothing and jewelry had been stolen; their relatives are understandably reluctant to bring wearing apparel, therefore, and many patients wear ill-fitting second-hand clothing that has been collected from charity. Some are dressed only in robes and slippers, and on many occasions patients were observed walking barefooted. Because of their lack of personal clothing and their unwilling inattention to grooming, patients lack individuality; there is a "sameness" about them. Many have the look of prison inmates.

Patients at Pacific Manor look forward to morning coffee, when a volunteer serves coffee to those in the lounge, but patients who choose to remain in their room receive none. The aides do not see this service as their responsibility; they feel it should be handled by the activity director. She has delegated this task, in turn, to a volunteer who serves only the thirty to forty patients who are in the lounge. Day after day I carried coffee to patients who had remained in their rooms; they accepted it gratefully, thanked me profusely, and knew, of course, that in my absence they would have received none.

Visiting: Family-Patient Relationships

Both institutions have flexible visiting hours; visitors may come at any time and stay for as long as they wish. There are many visitors at Pacific

Manor and Scottsdale; however, there are noticeable differences in the nature of the visiting. First, on some occasions friends and relatives brought children to visit the elderly at Scottsdale; children were never among the visitors at Pacific Manor. Second, although there were a few patients whose relatives did not visit them at Scottsdale, the majority had relatives and friends who seemed to enjoy coming and often stayed for a long time. At Pacific Manor, by contrast, visitors rushed in, stayed briefly, and were gone. A staff nurse who has worked at Pacific Manor for 12 years confirmed this observation: "75 percent of them make very short visits. Take Mrs. Curtis; her son [a physician] wasn't visiting and he didn't bring her anything, so we called him and suggested that he bring her a little treat now and then. So one day he came in with a little sack with a few cookies, kissed her on the forehead, and after about three or four minutes said, 'well, I have to get back to the office now.' That's no visit," the nurse objected. Another patient, whose daughter lived in the city, was visited so infrequently that for months the staff did not know she had a daughter. Of the eighty-five patients at Pacific Manor, only about eight have relatives who visit regularly, stay for lengthy visits, and bring small gifts.

The absence of children and the brevity and infrequency of visits may be explained by the conditions within the institution and by how patients feel about their institutionalization. Scottsdale is a very pleasant, comfortable facility; Pacific Manor is depressing and unpleasant. Patients at Scottsdale receive good care. "Their families know they are well cared for," said Sister Michael. "They know they are getting the best of care and that they are happy here." But at Pacific Manor relatives were often distressed by the lack of care yet felt helpless to change the situation. One woman had talked to everyone from the orderly to the administrator because her father needed help in walking. However, the staff would not help him walk; "We don't have time," they declared.

At Scottsdale the question "How do you find it here?" received a positive reply from every patient (the mean was 4.8):

> "It is a very happy place; I have never been lonely since I came. The nurses are very nice and the patients are very nice. I am as happy here as I have ever been anywhere."

> "I think it is the best hospital of its kind; we have a certain amount of freedom that you don't get in many hospitals."

"Smashing! It couldn't be better; I wouldn't leave here for anything!"

"It's a lovely place; it's nae my cup of tea to be in any hospital, but generally the care is good here."

"It is a very good hospital—when you have to be here for the rest of your life—I think it is about the best one you could find. We can get outside and go for runs [car rides]."

"Oh, lovely, fine, it is all very good, and we are very well fed."

"Very good, very good. I was at another hospital for a wee while, but it is much better here."

By contrast, at Pacific Manor the mean was 2.7 in response to the same question. Although there were some positive replies—such as, "It is very nice here; they are all good to me"; "I like it; I always feel at home with the girls and I know they like me"—the majority of patients were unhappy, and their responses indicated dissatisfaction with their living conditions:

"I don't like it because there is nothing to do but lay in bed and wait for time to pass."

"I don't like it here. If I could get a different place, I would leave."

"It is not so good—too lonesome. I don't know many people and I have visitors only once in a while."

"I don't like it much. I don't like it and don't dislike it. I make the best of it."

"I am very unhappy here. I don't like it here. They are not nice to sick old people. It costs $1,000 a month; that's a lot of money."

"I haven't been very happy here. I have to fend for myself. They have rules and some of them get bossy. I have been unhappy here."

Judging from these responses, one might hypothesize that, because the patients are unhappy, it is painful for relatives to visit; as a result they avoid an emotionally unpleasant experience by making infrequent and brief visits. One relative explained, "It breaks my heart to see my father here."

Institutional life for Scottish patients allows them more choice, freedom, and independence than it does for their American counterparts. They have a choice of food and films they would like to see, they elect officers for their social club, and they have money to purchase sundry items at a shop within the hospital. Their lives more closely approximate the life of an elderly person in the community. They are involved in productive activities, they go into the community for dinners and social events, and they are encouraged to spend time at home with their families.

But the elderly at Pacific Manor have little choice, freedom, or independence. They have no choice of food or entertainment; because of the danger of theft they cannot keep personal belongings or money in their rooms, and there is little opportunity to engage in activities of their choice. Their environment is restricted and narrow; they are isolated from the culture of the society without.

4

Staff-Patient
Interaction
at Pacific Manor

The preceding chapters contrasted the daily activities of patients in the two institutions. We have seen that the elderly at Scottsdale have more autonomy, live in a more "homelike" environment, and appear to be happy and content; while at Pacific Manor, patients have less freedom, live in a more austere, limiting environment, and express much discontent with their lives.

In this chapter I deal primarily with staff-patient interaction at Pacific Manor. In part this is so because I did not see significant problems in staff-patient interaction at Scottsdale and in part because I have more complete data from the American institution. As the reader will note, my reaction to the staff-patient interaction at Pacific Manor, on the whole, is negative. The facts I discuss should not be hidden; however, there are extenuating circumstances that should be noted. At Pacific Manor employees are grossly underpaid compared to staff in acute-care institutions. Although some are poorly qualified and would have difficulty obtaining employment in other institutions, their substandard pay and lack of professional competence suggests that they have a poor self-image; we cannot expect sympathetic and high-quality care from such personnel. Caring for the disabled elderly is physically and emotionally demanding. Because the work is hard and the pay inadequate, morale is low and the desire to retaliate comes forth all too easily. These conditions may contribute to the significant difference in patient care I observed in the American and Scottish institutions. At Scottsdale, on the whole, patients were treated kindly and with respect, but at Pacific Manor employees frequently were authoritarian and indifferent in their dealings with patients and showed little concern for their dignity and individual rights. The principal problems I encountered at Pacific Manor might be described as infantilization, depersonalization, dehumanization, and victimization.

Infantilization

Infantilization is the act of treating older people like children. It includes such behavior as scolding incontinent patients, addressing the elderly in casual or familiar terms, and dressing them in childish attire (Jaeger and Simmons 1970:38).

At Pacific Manor there were innumerable incidents of staff treating the residents like children. Authoritarian scoldings of the aged by staff were common. For example, one day a nurse aide walked into the lounge and, seeing a puddle of water on the floor, asked loudly, "Who wet the floor?" Pointing her finger at one woman, she inquired in an accusing voice, "Did you wet the floor?" Very embarrassed at being singled out as the culprit, the patient replied, "Why, no, it wasn't me." Staff frequently command patients in a parental voice: "Shut up!"; "Stay in your chair!"; "Go to your place for lunch"; "I want you to go in and put on a dress, now get dressed!"; and "Sit down, Grace." Such commands are often accompanied by gestures, such as pointing a finger at the aged person, forcibly taking him by the arm, or "leading" him to a chair. On some occasions, if patients do not comply, a threat is issued. Mrs. Garland, contrary to the directions of the activity director, repeatedly got up from her chair during a musical program. Later, the activity director asked one of the nurses, "What's the matter with Mrs. Garland today that she can't sit still?" The nurse explained the patient was anxious and agitated because her sons were away on vacation and had not been in to visit. "Oh," replied the activity director, laughingly, "Well, I told her if she didn't stay put, I would make her stand in the hall."

Staff of all ages and at all levels address patients by their Christian names or in familiar terms such as "Nana," "Mother," "Honey," or "Baby." One registered nurse habitually addresses all patients as "Honey": "Time for your blood pressure, Honey," "time for your pill, Honey."

Using this approach, she offered medication to a patient; he refused it. Without further verbal persuasion, she restrained both his arms so he could not resist and forced the medication into his mouth, saying "Come on now, Honey, take your pills." After she left the room, he spat the pills into the wastepaper basket.

I also observed that some patients had stuffed animals at their bedside and one woman continually held onto a stuffed doll. Upon inquiring, I learned that a registered nurse had given the stuffed animals to the patients for Christmas. One mentally impaired woman had been talking about her children, and the doll was given to her as a child substitute. However, others who received stuffed animals were not mentally impaired. "They need something soft and cuddly to hold onto," offered the nurse. I was sitting in the lounge one day when this nurse went off duty and heard her say to the patients as she passed through the lounge: "Bye, darlings, I'll see you all in the morning."

Perhaps the most blatant expression of the infantilizing treatment of the aged appears in the office of the director of nursing service. While discussing the number of patients with me, the director pointed to a directory on the wall. I was astonished to see the names of the male patients printed on blue labels and the female patients' names on pink labels. (For those not familiar with hospital routine, male infants' cribs in a nursery bear blue labels, and pink labels designate female infants' cribs.)

Of course, infantilization of the aged is objectionable and harmful. It offends their self-esteem, tends to promote regressive traits such as incontinence, increases dependency, and undermines any remaining sense of dignity and self-worth (Jaeger and Simmons 1970:48). Why, then, do staff persist in this behavior? Gresham (1976) proposes that an essential part of infantilization is a socialization process whereby the aged, who are seen by society as roleless and without status, are cast into the role of children. Henry (1964:443) suggests that personnel in institutions do not understand the aged, cannot empathize with them, and consequently gloss over everything by treating them as "confused babies." Many of the institutionalized aged at Pacific Manor, because of their multiple physical and mental disabilities, are dependent upon staff for total care. Their needs are similar to those of dependent children; it is quite likely therefore that dependence is associated with infancy and childhood. But their dependency does not justify treating the aged like children. Any person who is ill or disabled is dependent on others for basic needs; and although staff in acute-care hospitals may patronize the adult patient, certainly, infantilization as described above is seldom practiced.

I propose that infantilization of the elderly occurs because staff who have no professional training and who are professionally unsure of themselves find it advantageous to establish a "parent-child" relationship with the aged rather than an "adult-adult" relationship. When patients are treated like children, staff do not have to take their life-long accomplishments into consideration, and they can more easily exercise their authority. Commands can be given and must be obeyed without question; patients do not participate in decisions about when to eat, take medications, and go to bed. Their absolute authority gives care-givers control and simplifies their work and routine. To illustrate: Mrs. Levine, an intelligent woman, receives a diuretic pill three times a week. She realizes this tablet causes an increase in urinary output and has asked the nurse to withhold it on the day she has her hair shampooed; she is afraid she will be incontinent while having her hair done. For her own convenience, however, the "medication nurse" insists that Mrs. Levine take the pill when she is making her rounds; she will neither leave the pill at the bedside and trust Mrs. Levine to take it, nor will she return with it at a later time. "She just does not understand, and she forces me to take it," complained Mrs. Levine, "so when she leaves the room, I throw it away." (Staff attitudes, such as these, reflect the attitudes of the greater society; in the media, for example, aged people are often portrayed as senile, dependent, and infantile in behavior.)

Depersonalization

Depersonalization has been defined as "The process of depriving an individual of the factors that attach him to the social system" (Henry 1973:24). Depersonalization is the loss of personality, individuality, and sense of identity; it is what follows when people are treated with indifference, as if they have no value and are of no significance. All events that bind one to the social system are "personalizing"; conversely, everything that detaches one can be called "depersonalizing." The nature of attachment varies through time and is usually related to the economic and symbolic contributions a person makes to the culture. The person who contributes is readily contained within the social system and society responds positively, but it tends to expel from the social system the person who no longer contributes. In our culture the aged who are unable to care for themselves often are viewed as having lost the right to personality; and from a functional point of view, institutions for the aged have become a mechanism for depersonalization. Depersonalization occurs through symbolic means, through deprivation of individual choice and routinized care, and through deprivation of protection (Henry 1973:28–33).

Depersonalization Through Symbolic Means

Individuals are attached to the social system by its symbols; communication, both verbal and nonverbal, is essential for exchanging positive and negative responses with others. Addressing people improperly, ignoring them, or failing to communicate with them at all have depersonalizing effects (Henry 1973:28). On one occasion, Mrs. Garvey, a gentle 85-year-old woman, was sitting in the lounge; as a nurse aide walked by, Mrs. Garvey said, "Good morning." The aide did not reply. Another aide walked in and again Mrs. Garvey said, "Good morning." Again there was no reply. This scene occurred repeatedly; staff walked by as if she were not there. After several minutes, other patients gathered in the lounge and Mrs. Garvey said, "Good morning, everybody"; two women responded. I walked over and said, "Good morning, Mrs. Garvey; how are you today?" "Good morning, darling," she replied. "You are a nice lady. Thank you for stopping. These people don't know what it is like to grow old; they forget that some day they are going to be old, too."

Nursing staff do not always address patients by their proper names, rather they refer to them as "the newly admitted patient," "the patient in 10A," or "the woman with the colostomy." Personnel also contrive nicknames for some patients: 95-year-old Mrs. Buckingham is called "Bucky," and another woman is called "Nana-Banana."

Staff frequently ignore patients' calls for help. Patients put on their call light, and when this signal is disregarded, they begin to call for help. "Help, help, will someone please help me," pleads one patient. The staff pass by the door as if they do not hear her. A visitor walks by and the patient calls, "Help, gentleman, please help me." Another woman begins to call for help; an aide sitting at the end of the hallway shouts, "Eleanor, you be quiet!" The patient continues to call. "Eleanor, if I have to come down there you are going to be sorry; now shut up!" I walked into the room and found a blind woman crying; she wanted to go to the bathroom and lie down because she was tired. When this was reported to the charge nurse, she asked the aide to help the patient. "I know what she wants," replied the aide. After 10 or 15 minutes, she grudgingly went to the aid of the patient.

Mr. Bonner, a 91-year-old widower, provides a final example of depersonalization through deprivation of communication. He had been admitted for physical therapy following a fractured hip; prior to this injury he had been living alone in his home. While walking down the hallway I heard him say, "Help me to die, help me to die." "Why are you saying that," I asked. "I might as well die," he shrugged. "I just lie here. Everybody walks by; they don't pay any attention to me. I would like to go home so I can see my neighbors," he went on. "Even if I don't talk with them, I can see them go by." Mr. Bonner tried to alleviate the loneliness and isolation by singing to himself. Day after day he sat quietly humming and singing. After finishing my field work, I went back to see some of the patients and asked about Mr. Bonner. "He doesn't sing any more," said the orderly. Three weeks later they told me he had died.

Depersonalization Through Routinized Care and Deprivation of Individual Choice

Patient care becomes routinized when it is given in the simplest and most expeditious way. Individual differences are not taken into account and staff can perform their duties with minimum communication, in assembly-line fashion. For instance, patients do not select food; the same menu is served to everyone at the same time. And a monthly group birthday party at Pacific Manor is an efficient way of giving token, rather than individual, recognition to the aged. At Scottsdale, by comparison, patients have a selective menu; and if they wish to celebrate their birthday, friends or relatives bring cake and sherry for the staff and other patients on the ward.

To be fair, I must add that routinized care for the benefit of staff was also practiced at Scottsdale. Patients frequently complain because they have to go to bed for the evening between 2 P.M. and 4 P.M. The employees maintain this is necessary because there is minimal help on duty between 4 P.M. and 10 P.M.; and because many patients need help in getting into bed, this task must be completed before the personnel from the day shift go off duty. Although this routine is seen by the staff as necessary, it is depersonalizing as well as infantilizing for patients to be put to bed at an early hour.

Depersonalization by Deprivation of Protection

A social system must provide protection for its members; if that protection is not given, the unprotected feel that "nobody cares." For those who must depend on others for their basic needs, protection means not only freedom from harm and injury but freedom from all that threatens their physical survival (Henry: 1973:32).

Patients at Pacific Manor made numerous complaints of theft, a point I will discuss in detail under the heading "Victimization." In addition to being victimized by staff, patients were also victimized by each other. Several reported that food and clothing were taken from their rooms by confused patients who wandered indiscriminately from one room to another. Mrs. Levine was missing a dress and later saw another patient wearing it. On another occasion she found the same woman in her room, eating pastry left for Mrs. Levine by her family. She reported these incidents to the staff, who said they were helpless to control such behavior. Staff not only were indifferent to this type of problem but also saw humor in such situations. Two patients (roommates) were being discussed in morning report. "Mrs. Robinson is capable of eating by herself," said the nurse, "but she waits for someone to come and help her, and while she is waiting, Mrs. Fong jumps out of bed and eats the food right off her tray." The staff laughed at the incident and joked that Mrs. Fong is so hungry she eats everything but the plate. Later, I learned that Mrs. Fong was a "very brittle diabetic" (her diabetes was difficult to control with insulin injections) and the doctor had been increasing her insulin in an attempt to keep her urine free from sugar. Meanwhile, she was stealing food from other patients because the insulin made her abnormally hungry.

The health of patients sometimes is threatened because they are not dressed warmly. Many sit for hours in short hospital gowns, without robes and slippers, while waiting to be bathed. Patients feel threatened because of lack of medical care (as will be seen in Chapter 6). Mrs. Tyler repeatedly talked about how unhappy she was with the care her physician provided. Before her admission, she had undergone surgery for cancer of the tongue. Part of her tongue and mandible had been removed, and she lived in fear that there would be a recurrence of the cancer. Her doctor seldom came; when he did visit, she inquired about the lump in her neck. "That's not my field," he replied. She was terrified of this newly found lump because an earlier one had proven cancerous, and she said to me, "If you ever have a lump in your neck, even if it is painless, be sure to have it checked." I reported her concern to the nurse in charge, who replied, "Mrs. Tyler likes hospitals and is scared to death of cancer." Clearly, it is terrifying and threatening for patients to feel they need medical care and have no control over when they will see a doctor. "They said my doctor will come when he feels like it," Mrs. Crawford mused, "but I don't like that attitude."

The individual emerges in social interaction; moreover, people need continuous confirmation of self through interaction with others (Mead 1934). Meaningful social interaction requires ongoing relationships with others. The lack of patient-staff communication, along with a relatively high turnover of patients as well as professional staff at Pacific Manor (see Chapter 6), makes it difficult if not impossible for patients to establish meaningful relationships. When there is no opportunity for continuing relationships, people tend to withdraw from social interaction (Henry 1973:33). Townsend (1962:329) notes that, when the elderly are deprived of intimate family relationships and cannot find substitutes, a gradual process of depersonalization follows. Patients become apathetic, lack initiative, talk little, and withdraw into a private world of fantasy.

Many of the patients at Pacific Manor were withdrawn and apathetic, there was little socializing among them, and few developed friendships. Some who saw each other daily did not know one another by name. "I don't go out of my way to meet people," explained Mrs. Levine. Another, Mrs. Arny, was paralyzed from her waist down and never left her room. Miss Knutson, a rather anxious patient, paced the halls and often stopped in for a brief visit. But while talking with Mrs. Arny, I was surprised to learn she did not know the name of this woman who had been stopping by to see her. While I visited with patients in the physical therapy room, one patient pointed to another and said, "I feel sorry for that one; he lost his wife two days before their fiftieth wedding anniversary." "What is his name," I inquired. "I don't know," she answered. Yet at Scottsdale there was a great deal of social interaction among patients: they not only were acquainted with one another but strong friendships had developed between some, and a feeling of "community" was present. When Mrs. Ross was confined to her bed for a few days, others noticed her absence at coffee, inquired of her, and her good friend, Mrs. Maury, who could hardly walk, insisted upon visiting her for afternoon tea.

Dehumanization

"Dehumanization is the loss of humanity" (Vail 1966:5); it is what follows when a person is treated insensitively, callously, and when he is subjected to experiences that are an affront to his dignity and sense of self-worth. To dehumanize another is to deprive him of human attributes such as compassion, understanding, and kindness.

There is a fine distinction between depersonalization and dehumanization, and although both have detrimental effects, the latter is more serious. Whereas in depersonalization a loss of personality and individuality takes place, dehumanization, or treating a person as a nonhuman (perhaps as an animal or as an inanimate object), is even more devastating.

Dehumanization Through Insensitivity to Patients' Needs

As will be noted in Chapter 5, many of the institutionalized elderly are disabled and dependent upon others for basic needs such as eating, dressing, bathing, and voiding. Yet it is difficult for the elderly to accept dependence as a permanent condition. So to minimize feelings of dependence, staff should attend to their needs with kindness and understanding yet help them remain as independent as possible.

At Pacific Manor the way staff attended to patients' needs was frequently dehumanizing. Eating, for example, is a social experience as well as a nutritional necessity. At Scottsdale staff sat and talked with patients while feeding them; and when they were short of help and did not have time to feed patients leisurely, staff members complained loudly that it was unpleasant for patients when staff had to feed two or three at once. By contrast, at Pacific Manor personnel stood silently in front of patients and hurriedly fed them. On one occasion Mrs. Garvey, who usually ate independently, had not eaten her lunch. Rather than inquiring why she had not eaten and encouraging her to eat, the aide filled a spoon with ground meat and mashed potatoes and forced it into her mouth. She repeatedly placed large spoonfuls of food into Mrs. Garvey's mouth and commanded her to "Eat, eat, eat!" While the patient protested she could eat no more, the aide ignored her objections. Only when Mrs. Garvey said, "I am going to vomit" did the aide stop forcing her to eat.

Having personal clothing contributes to one's individuality and self-esteem. As discussed in Chapter 3, many patients at Pacific Manor do not have personal clothing, and what is provided for them is ill-fitting, unpressed, and inappropriate. The available clothing (contributed by charitable organizations or left behind by previous patients) is stuffed in large cardboard boxes; no attempt is made to keep it neat or pressed. When someone needs a shirt or dress, attendants pull out whatever they can find; if the appropriate piece of attire is not available, a substitute is made. Mrs. White, an attractive 78-year-old woman who normally sat in a wheelchair clad in a sweater and slip, had to wear a bathrobe tied backwards around her waist to simulate a skirt when the therapist came to help her walk. To lack underclothes or to have clothes put on backwards is also dehumanizing for the elderly. Robes often are put on in this way, staff informed me, to decrease the amount of work involved in changing an incontinent patient and to decrease the amount of laundry. If robes are put on backwards and not tucked under, they are not soiled when patients are incontinent.

Many of the dehumanizing experiences at Pacific Manor centered around bathing and elimination. Exposing patients' genitals, bathing men and women simultaneously in the same shower room, and creating a situation in which the elderly, owing to lack of help and attention, defecate and urinate on the floor illustrate an insensitivity to patients' needs and are an affront to their dignity. At Scottsdale patients were never exposed; when attending them, staff carefully drew bedside curtains and closed the door. On any given day at Pacific Manor, one could walk down the hallway and observe patients sitting in chairs or lying in bed unclothed. On one occasion a patient sitting in the hallway was incontinent. The nurse aide stood him up, instructed him to hold onto the wall railing, and changed his trousers in the public corridor without regard for his modesty. Another patient, Mr. Thomas, always sat in a particular location in the hallway. One evening I saw him struggling to get out of his wheelchair. Sensing he needed a urinal, I called the nurse. "Oh, that's all right," she assured me. "Don't worry about him; he has two spots right here in the hallway where he urinates every day." The expression on my face was one of shock and disbelief as I watched this man publicly urinate on the carpet in the hallway. "What's the matter," laughed the nurse, "is it too much for you?"

Exposing the genitals and urinating in public is a violation of a cultural taboo. When such actions are permitted and accepted as a matter of course, they degrade and dehumanize those who violate the taboo as well as those who must observe such behavior, for the person violating the

taboo obviously is no longer considered a part of the social system. That
is, he is no longer considered a significant member of the human race
(Henry 1973:31). It is as though, by dehumanizing the elderly, the staff
revokes their status as human beings and relegates them to the status of
animals. After all, animals, not humans, expose their genitals and defecate
in public. For the elderly who have been brought up under strict codes of
modesty, violation of these norms is the ultimate indignity they must
suffer in old age.

Forcing patients to wait endlessly for assistance with the necessities of
life is also dehumanizing. Patients at Pacific Manor and their families constantly report that staff refuse to help them go to the bathroom when
necessary. Mr. Daniels asked to be taken to the bathroom; the orderly
replied that the attendant in charge of his care was at lunch and that Mr.
Daniels would have to wait 30 minutes until he returned. Because Mr.
Daniels was unable to wait, he was incontinent and highly embarrassed
when his daughter arrived for a visit, only to find his clothing soiled. I
asked Mrs. LaSalle, a patient whose left side was paralyzed, what was the
most difficult adjustment when she came to the nursing home. "Having
to wait two hours for someone to help me to the bathroom," she responded. "How can you possibly wait that long," I inquired. "You just
have to." Another patient, Mrs. Arny, elaborated, "You have to wait
longer in the evening for help; it is hard on your morale, but there is no
sense in losing patience with the nurses. It is best just to keep it inside; I
just feel angry inside. Sometimes when I wet the bed they say, 'you just lie
in it now.'" In both Pacific Manor and Scottsdale, patients who were able
to use the toilet themselves without assistance valued this ability highly
and mentioned it often. At Scottsdale Mrs. Duncan spoke with obvious
pride: "I can get myself to the bathroom and back, and I am really glad
about that." At Pacific Manor Mrs. Levine was also partially content: "I
only weighed 66 pounds when I came in here, and I couldn't do anything
for myself. Now, I can dress myself and go to the bathroom and I am
happy about that. It takes me all morning, but I have nothing else to do."

When adults can no longer attend to their basic needs, that is a frightening experience—it suggests they are regressing to a dependent, childlike
state. Staff should be extremely sensitive to the fact that this is a threatening experience for the aged and do everything possible to preserve their
privacy and dignity when attending to their needs.

Dehumanization Through Lack of Compassion, Kindness, and Understanding

A personal relationship between staff and the elderly in long-term-care institutions is desirable and essential. Many of the aged are experiencing multiple losses and need someone to listen and try to understand the depth of their loneliness. It is difficult, if not impossible, to comprehend the loneliness they feel over the loss of friends and relatives. In both institutions patients repeatedly expressed sadness over such losses. "I'm all alone in the world," said one of the Scottish women; "I haven't a soul in the world." Mrs. Boske, a patient at Pacific Manor shared this feeling: "All of my friends have died, and I am so lonely; my husband died 35 years ago. But I guess that's what happens when one is so presumptuous as to live so long," she added with a resigned smile. She is a strong woman, and her comment suggests that she blames only herself for her circumstances. Some patients are not as strong as Mrs. Boske. Many desperately need the kindness, support, and compassion of staff to help them through a difficult phase in their lives. Ninety-nine-year-old Mr. White, a bachelor, is alone in the world. His only visitor is a woman who has been appointed by the court to be his guardian. "Pull up a chair and sit down," he immediately suggested as I entered the room. "I am glad when someone comes to visit me, and I would never chase a lady out of the room. No one ever comes in." As I started to offer him a glass of water, I found the pitcher empty. I filled it with ice water and gave him some. "Thank you, that was wonderful," he said. "I can't go after it and I can't even pour it in the glass anymore. One boy used to come and give me water, but nobody comes any more. They are all so cruel to me. I asked a nurse for a towel to clean my glasses and she handed me a wet one. I said, 'this towel is wet,' and she said 'it's good enough for you.' Some of the boys who mop the floor are nice to me, but the nurses don't talk to me. They walk by the door, but nobody stops to talk with me." Mr. White does not require a great deal of nursing care, but he does need kindness and companionship.

Mr. White, however, is not as desperate as 87-year-old Mr. Fuller. Mr. Fuller's wife was terminally ill when she was admitted to Pacific Manor, and because he did not want to leave her, he asked to be admitted too. The staff considerately placed the two in a double room (in the Scottish institution, one couple was separated into male and female wards). On the day of their admission, the following notation was made on Mr. Fuller's chart: "Cries easily because of wife's illness. Doctor has *not* told him wife may die soon." Within a few days Mrs. Fuller died; her husband was grief stricken. He attended her funeral and the doctor noted on the chart: "Patient withstood funeral of wife—barely"; he ordered a dose of Valium for him.

Mr. and Mrs. Fuller had been married for over 50 years, had no children, and were very dependent on each other for companionship in their old age. In the weeks following his wife's death, Mr. Fuller was depressed and sat alone in his room. After some time he went into the lounge, where he met Mrs. Guido; she was grieving over the death of her only daughter. A friendship developed, and often the two would sit quietly holding hands; sometimes they cried softly together. This conduct was quickly noticed by the staff, who called me into the lounge one day, pointed at them, and said, "It looks like we have a romance here; Mr. Fuller has found a girlfriend already. It sure doesn't take long, does it?" Unfortunately for Mr. Fuller, Mrs. Guido was transferred to another nursing home. After she left he remained alone in his room. Although the "activity plan" on his chart noted he was a recent widower and suggested "Staff should be supportive and allow him to cry and express his sorrow," during three months of field work not once did I observe a staff member offer support. Knowing he was alone and depressed, I visited him each time I went to the nursing home. During each visit he cried over the loss of his wife and was fearful he would lose his home because of the cost of being institutionalized (he was not eligible for Medicare or Medicaid). He was also tearful when he talked about maltreatment from the staff. "I have always treated everybody nice," he mentioned. "I never knew there were people like this. They beat me. Those big men come in and throw me around, and at nighttime when I call for help, they call me a bad boy." He began to cry and then blurted out, "I would like to commit suicide; I would like to die, that is the best." As I left the room he said, "Thanks a million; you have helped me a lot." Alarmed at the severe degree of his depression, I discussed his condition with the charge nurse and asked if she could arrange for someone to spend some time with him. "He is very depressed over the loss of his wife," I explained. "Yeah, I guess he is depressed," she agreed. "He's been that way ever since he came in here. I don't know why the doctor doesn't order more Valium for him." There was no understanding on her part of his need for compassion and companionship.

The physical abuse described by Mr. Fuller was alluded to by others as well. However, patients were reluctant to discuss the subject openly, for they were fearful their conversations might be relayed "to the heads." Often while I talked with patients, they appeared anxious and apprehensive and would worry, "This won't go to the heads, will it?" Although verbal abuse was common, I did not observe physical abuse.

Victimization

Victimization is the act of being harmed or made to suffer by the actions of others. During the past several years, much attention has been focused on criminal victimization of the elderly, and in 1975 "The National Conference on Crime Against the Elderly" was held in Washington, D.C. (Goldsmith and Goldsmith 1976). Issues addressed at this conference included the vulnerability of the aged (physical, economic, and environmental factors that increase susceptibility to criminal attack), robbery, purse snatching, and fraudulent activities against the elderly. Recent figures on crime rates indicate that the elderly are victimized no more frequently than other age groups (Cook et al. 1978); nevertheless, more than any other age group, they suffer painful losses at the hands of criminal offenders.

Although some attention is being given to the problem of the victimization of the elderly in the community at large, to the best of my knowledge the issue of victimization of the institutionalized aged has not been explored. Yet this subgroup of the elderly is the most vulnerable of all. They often are disabled, many are alone and have no one to whom they can turn for help, and they are dependent upon those who victimize them for their care.

Theft of Personal Belongings

Broadly speaking, infantilization, depersonalization, and dehumanization are forms of victimization that are psychologically harmful to the aged. Still, at Pacific Manor theft of personal possessions is an overt type of victimization; the theft of patients' food, clothing, money, jewelry, and other personal belongings is common. As mentioned earlier, many patients do not like the institutional diet and try to supplement it with food from friends and relatives. But because of theft, it is nearly impossible for them to keep food in their possession. If they place perishable goods in the refrigerator, invariably they are taken by the staff. As a result, many patients asked their families to bring only nonperishable food that they can keep hidden in their rooms. Even this does not always prove successful; patients do not have a locked cupboard. A few of the more resourceful ones have obtained small bags that they keep with them at all times. "Mrs. Levine taught me how to keep my personal articles and food in this bag," confided Mrs. LaVelle. "The handles fit nicely over the arm of the wheelchair, and I can keep it with me at all times." Despite the lack of a secure place, patients were extremely clever in hiding their belongings. Mrs. O'Sullivan always had a bottle of wine in her room. The staff knew she had it and were amazed no one had been able to locate it.

In addition to food, patients also talked about other possessions they had lost. Mrs. O'Sullivan said that during her institutionalization three coin purses, a billfold, flashlight, candy, and even her earplugs had been stolen. Mrs. Crawford's portable radio and a $40 robe her niece had sent her for Christmas were also stolen. Her vision is so poor she cannot read, so she depends on the radio for entertainment and to keep her informed. "I don't mean to sound snobbish," she told me, "but I like to know what is going on in the world, and the radio keeps me in touch." She had another one brought in and asked the maintenance man to secure it to the bed with a heavy chain. The daughter of another patient said, "Everything goes here; that's par for the course. I can't keep my father in underclothes, and when I ask the staff about missing clothing, they say it has been lost in the laundry."

The staff take no responsibility for theft. A family preparing to take their elderly aunt home was upset because her suitcase and three new bedjackets were missing. When they complained to the charge nurse, she was nonplussed: "Well, it's hard for us to keep track of everything." When another patient had been transferred to an acute-care hospital, his cash and radio were left behind. "We should lock up that radio in the nurses' station," suggested one staff member. "No, it should be in a safer place," the charge nurse corrected. "A lot of people have a key to that cupboard in the nurses' station, and I don't want to be responsible for it. It is bad enough his money was taken; there was money in his billfold when he left and now it is flat as a pancake. God help us if he ever gets well and comes back and finds his money gone."

Some patients warn others of the theft problem and give their valuables to relatives before admission. Mrs. Crawford, Mrs. Levine, and Mrs. O'Sullivan gave all of their jewelry to their daughters and nieces, and they were wearing "dime store wedding rings." "It just makes me sick that I can't wear my jewelry," said Mrs. Levine, "but I could never keep it here because it would be taken." Americans value and take pride in personal possessions; often they are symbolic of life events. It is appalling that the environment of our institutions for the aged is such that the elderly must spend their last days deprived of the pleasure they would get from these personal items. "It's not having any of the amenities that is so hard to take," Mrs. Levine went on. "I would like to have my tea in a nice china cup, sit up to a table for dinner, and have some of my personal things around me."

Theft was absolutely unheard of at Scottsdale, where patients enjoyed wearing their jewelry and personal clothing. Mrs. McDonald, tearfully but proudly, showed me a medal her deceased daughter had won in a swimming event; she always wore it to the monthly meeting of the "Social Club."

The prevalence of theft has a harmful effect on the aged; they live in fear that their few possessions will be taken. It is frightening, of course, for them to have to depend for care on those who are stealing their belongings. Ninety-year-old Mrs. Snyder kept apples in her room. "If I eat an apple every day, it keeps my bowels regular," she elaborated. "One day I walked into my room and an orderly was eating my only apple." "Did you say anything to him?" I asked. "Oh, no!" she replied. "He might have hit me! I just said to myself that I hoped he would get a tummyache from it."

Factors That Contribute to Theft

Two major factors within the social structure of the institution have been identified that contribute to the victimization of the aged at Pacific Manor. First, there is a greater social distance between staff and patients at Pacific Manor than at Scottsdale; and second, the administrative staff take no responsibility for the problem.

Social Distance at Pacific Manor

Although a few staff members have developed personal relationships with patients, the majority have not. They communicate minimally with them, are distant in their relationships, and even on social occasions, such as the monthly birthday party, do not join in the festivities. The kitchen help and volunteers serve refreshments to the patients while the nursing staff sit in the hallway and eat cake and ice cream. The personnel at Scottsdale, by comparison, are more personally involved with patients (some, on their days off, brought their children or grandchildren to visit the elderly); they socialize, at least monthly, at the Scottsdale Social Club. And because the staff at Pacific Manor infantilize, depersonalize, and de-humanize patients, they are not likely to develop personal relationships with them. It becomes easy for staff to steal from a "childlike, nonperson, nonhuman" who has no rights.

Lack of Administrative Responsibility for Theft at Pacific Manor

Responsibility is an instrument used by societies to help maintain social control (Schafer 1977:150). When it is apparent that no one is responsible for the protection of those who are unable to protect themselves, the weak and handicapped become easy prey. The nonprofessional staff at Pacific Manor know, first, that the administration takes no responsibility for the problem of theft; they have heard administrators and professional staff tell families they cannot be held accountable for lost articles. Second, they also know theft is not a priority with management; their primary responsibility is to make a profit for the owner of the institution, and stealing from patients does not interfere with profit making. Third, the rapid turnover of administrative staff also contributes to the problem. At Pacific Manor the auxiliary personnel wield the power; they know they will be there long after the administrators have moved on to other jobs. Lastly, they know they have nothing to lose. Because their salaries are low and it is difficult to hire staff, they are not threatened with the loss of their jobs.

The foregoing discussion provides some insight into the problem of theft, but victimization of the institutionalized aged cannot be understood without an understanding of victimization of the aged in the community at large. And both must be looked at in the larger socio-cultural context in which the crime occurs. As mentioned earlier, crime against the elderly in the U.S. has become a major issue in social gerontology. At first glance it seems incredible that the elderly, many of whom are unable to retaliate, should be victimized, but in fact their helplessness makes them ideal vic-tims. Hentig (1948:438), a pioneer in the study of victims, classified them into categories that include minorities, immigrants, children, females, and the aged.

Old people, especially if they are physically and mentally weak, are ideal victims of predatory attack. Reiman (1976) proposes that certain groups in our society have been labeled "legitimate victims"; they are defective human beings, and the message conveyed by society is that victimization of these groups is not as objectionable as the victimization of "normal folks." As an example, he observes that public outrage is greater if a white student is shot than if a black student is the victim. Similarly, old people in America are viewed as substandard (Reiman 1976:79). In a youth-oriented culture, the aged are characterized as useless, dependent, physically and mentally weak, poor, and noncontributing; in short, they are a burden and a nuisance. Americans value independence and fear dependence; it follows then that if the aged do not "carry their own weight" they cannot be valued. This negative attitude toward the aged contributes to victimization of the elderly in the community as well as in institutions. If one lives in a society that does not value the aged, it becomes easy to victimize that group, and the institutionalized aged, a weakened and dependent group, become "captive victims" for predators.

5

Demographic Characteristics of the Residents

The last two chapters contrasted the quality of life offered in the two institutions and discussed the dehumanizing and depersonalizing treatment of the aged in the American nursing home. In the next three chapters, likely contributions to these differences will be considered, particularly the demographic characteristics of the aged in each institution, their medical and nursing care, and finally the historical differences in the organization and financing of health care in the two countries.

Average Age and Ratio of Men to Women

People in long-term-care institutions in the United States and Britain are very old, largely white, and predominantly women. In the United States the average age is 82 years, 96 percent are white, and women outnumber men three to one (Special Committee on Aging, United States Senate 1974). Patients at Pacific Manor conform fairly closely to this profile. Their average age is 83.5 years, 94 percent are white, and the ratio of women to men is 3.7 to 1. The most notable contrast at Scottsdale is the significantly lower mean age of only 72.5 years, 100 percent of the residents are white, and women outnumber men by a ratio of 4.3 to 1. Table 4 presents the mean age of males and females in each group as well as the number and percentages of patients in each age range.

Table 4. Number, sex, and percentage of patients in each age range

Age range	Pacific Manor				Scottsdale			
			Total				Total	
	Men	Women	No.	%	Men	Women	No.	%
40–49	0	0	0	0	2	3	5	5
50–59	0	2	2	2.3	3	13	16	16
60–69	1	3	4	4.7	3	9	12	13
70–79	5	20	25	29	3	19	22	23
80–89	7	30	37	44	6	21	27	28
90–99	5	12	17	20	1	13	14	15
Total	18	67	85	100%	18	78	96	100%

What calls for explanation in these statistics is the surprising difference of eleven years in the mean age of the residents in the two institutions, since the life-expectancy rates in the two countries are very similar (68.8 years for males and 75.1 for females in Britain versus 68.9 for males and 76.6 for females in the United States). Part of the difference can be explained by the fact that the Scottish institution has a large number of patients (23.6 percent) with multiple sclerosis, the majority of whom are under 65 years of age. Nevertheless, if patients under 65 years of age are omitted from a calculation of the mean age, the Scottish residents are still significantly younger: 76.6 years as compared to 83.5 years at Pacific Manor. At least two considerations may account for this difference. First, elderly people in the United States view admission to a nursing home with fear and hostility; they see it as a prelude to death (Shanas 1962; Butler 1975). Second, nursing home care is very costly, and some elderly people fear they will use all of their life savings and have to resort to welfare in their last days. For people who have been independent all of their lives, this prospect is of grave concern. In the city where this research was conducted, nursing home fees range from $992 to $2,852 per month; consequently, modest life savings can be quickly exhausted.

Perhaps because of these two fears, the elderly in the United States postpone admission to a nursing home and resort to institutional care only when the multiple disabilities of very advanced age (80 years and over) make living in the community absolutely impossible.

Race and Religion

Scotland is a homogeneous country; all of the patients at Scottsdale are white and about 97 percent belong to the Church of Scotland (Presbyterian). The remaining 3 percent are Roman Catholic. In contrast, Pacific Manor patients are religiously heterogeneous; 50 percent protestant, 29 percent Catholic, 11 percent Jewish and 10 percent express no religious preference. The religious background of the patients is of interest, primarily, because it suggests that although some religious organizations attempt to provide care for their members (i.e., Jewish and Catholic homes), they are unable to accommodate all those who need institutional care. For example, Jewish patients at Pacific Manor say there is a 2-year waiting list for admission to the Jewish home.

Pacific Manor is located in a metropolitan area in which there are large numbers of several minority groups. Despite this fact, 96 percent of the patients are white, two are Chinese, one Japanese, and two have Spanish surnames. The absence of minority patients may be explained by Pacific Manor's private ownership and high cost of care. The administration will not accept Medicaid patients; the lower economic status of some minority group members prohibits their admission, therefore. Proprietary nursing homes in this particular city are increasingly serving only privately supported patients. Nursing home owners and administrators maintain that Medicaid reimbursement rates (the state financed medical care program for the indigent) are not high enough to cover the cost of patient care; thus, they refuse to admit publicly financed patients.

At this point it is important to note that although the minority elderly could not afford to be admitted to Pacific Manor because of its high cost of care, virtually all of the nonprofessional and many of the professional staff were nonwhite. Hence, nonwhite caretakers are providing services to a nearly all white patient population. At Scottsdale, by comparison, patients and staff are religiously and racially homogeneous. Gottesman (1974) notes that in church-related facilities, such as the Jewish home and in another facility that had primarily black residents, black staff, and a black owner, the motivation to care for one's own was great.

The homogeneity of staff and patients at Scottsdale may contribute to a higher level of care, whereas the heterogeneity of staff and patients at Pacific Manor may account for a lower level of care. But I am hesitant to pursue this thesis because in acute-care facilities this same dissimilarity often exists and does not appear to be significant. I believe that with responsible professional leadership in the nursing home, ethnicity should not be an important factor.

Family Structure

As we have seen, people in long-term-care institutions are elderly, predominantly women, and largely white. Admission to a nursing home is partly contingent upon family structure. The likelihood of admission is greater if one is single, widowed, or divorced and without children; studies conclude that 50 percent of the institutionalized aged either have no living relatives or no viable relationship with distant relatives (Townsend 1965; Gottesman 1972; Special Committee on Aging, United States Senate 1974; Butler 1975).

The findings presented in this study confirm some but not all of these observations. The majority of the aged in both institutions are either single or widowed, with the exception of the Scottish men, 50 percent of whom are married. Table 5 shows the marital status of patients in each institution. The high number of married men is explained by the fact, as we have seen, that one-third of the males (four of the nine married men) at Scottsdale have advanced multiple sclerosis.

Also, as compared to circumstances at Pacific Manor, a very high percentage of the women in Scottsdale—40 percent—are single. The high mortality rate of British males during World War I and the emigration of young adult males during the early years of the twentieth century explain this phenomenon. Americans may find it difficult to believe just how many British women were affected by the high male mortality rates during World War I; however, several women at Scottsdale spoke of the loss of their loved one. "I lost my sweetheart in World War I and so I never

Table 5. Marital status of patients (in percentages)

Marital status	Scottsdale		Pacific Manor	
	Men	Women	Men	Women
Widowed	28	42	44	55.0
Single	22	40	31	30.0
Married	50	18	19	7.5
Divorced	0	0	6	7.5
Total	100%	100%	100%	100%

married," sighed a charming 97-year-old woman, "but don't you worry; I have had some good times too."

Unlike some of the studies mentioned above, which suggest that 50 percent of the elderly in long-term-care institutions are without living relatives, this study found the majority of the elderly in both institutions to have families. At Scottsdale 95 percent have living relatives, including children, brothers, sisters, nieces, and nephews; 54 percent have children. And at Pacific Manor 73 percent of the residents have living relatives, including 56 percent with children.

Thus, although the majority of the elderly have living relatives, other factors make institutionalization inevitable for them. Many children of the institutionalized aged, both in Scotland and the United States, live a great distance from their parents. At Scottsdale, for example, Mrs. Elwood's only daughter had married and emigrated to Canada. In some cases, the children of patients are themselves already elderly and may be in poor health. At Pacific Manor 93-year-old Mr. Sampson had been cared for at home by his daughter, a frail 70-year-old woman. Despite his multiple physical disabilities and slight mental impairment, she managed quite well until he fell and fractured his hip. While Mr. Sampson was recovering from his fractured hip, Ms. Sampson fell and fractured her right arm. These two accidents greatly multiplied the problem of caring for him at home and necessitated his institutionalization. Despite family status then, in some instances other factors are ultimately responsible for the institutionalization of the elderly.

Physical and Mental Health

Many residents in both institutions have multiple, chronic, organic, physical illnesses, often combined with some degree of mental impairment, which result in their inability to care for themselves. Most frequently, the mental and physical disabilities such as immobility, incontinence, and mental confusion finally necessitate institutionalization. Table 6 presents the physical disorders and functional disabilities of patients in both institutions.

In the United States, nursing homes provide care for a wide range of mentally and physically disabled people. In Britain, although some overlap occurs from institution to institution, a greater attempt is made to separate the elderly into appropriate accommodations, such as sheltered housing,

Table 6. Physical disabilities and functional disorders of patients (in percentages)

Physical Disabilities		
Category of disease	Scottsdale	Pacific Manor
Diseases of the circulatory system	41	51
Rheumatoid arthritis	20	12
Multiple sclerosis	25	0
Fractured hip	6	23
Diabetes mellitus	5	10
Other	3	4
Total	100%	100%

Functional Disorders		
Type of disorder	Scottsdale	Pacific Manor
Immobile	70	46
Walk with help	24	17
Walk unaided	6	37
Urinary incontinence	51	33
Urinary catheters	5	17
Mental impairment	45	72

residential homes, geriatric units, continuing care units, and psychogeriatric units.

Immobility

Immobility greatly increases the problems of the elderly and places a heavy burden on those who must care for them. The nonambulant patient requires much assistance in such things as dressing, bathing, using the toilet, and getting in and out of bed.

As documented in Table 6, the patients at Scottsdale are more physically disabled than the patients at Pacific Manor; however, it is important to note that the immobile patients were unable to walk prior to their admission. Their problems of immobility did not occur because of a lack of nursing care. Before admission, the elderly patients at Scottsdale have undergone extensive diagnostic examination, treatment, and rehabilitation;

and for the most part, only the severely disabled are admitted for long-term care. But at Pacific Manor some patients are admitted to the nursing home when they could be cared for in their homes if community services were available.

Mental Impairment

In both institutions a significant number of patients display some degree of mental impairment. The subject of brain failure (organic brain disorders) and functional brain disorders is complex, and a full discussion of the problem is neither within the scope of this study nor within the expertise of the author. However, mental impairment is a major contributor to the institutionalization of elderly people; indeed, the prevalence of mental disability in both the American and the Scottish patients warrants a brief discussion of the problem.

At Scottsdale 16 percent of the patients have a medical diagnosis of dementia (organic brain disorder). This figure contrasts sharply with the patient population at Pacific Manor, 42 percent of whom have a medical diagnosis of some type of mental disorder. In the American institution a wide variety of terms is used to describe mental impairment, such as organic brain disease, chronic brain syndrome, cerebral arteriosclerotic disease, senility, senile dementia, and cerebral insufficiency; chronic brain syndrome is the term most commonly used. In addition to the medical diagnosis, the nursing staff at Pacific Manor reports that 72 percent of the patients are confused; at Scottsdale the nursing staff reports that 45 percent of the patients have some degree of mental impairment. The chief geriatrician at Scottsdale confirmed the report of the nursing staff and said that approximately 40 percent of the patients show some evidence of brain failure but without important accompanying behavior problems.

Mental impairment in old age is a major problem in both the United States and Britain. Some studies in the United States report that 55 to 80 percent of long-term patients are mentally impaired (Special Committee on Aging, United States Senate 1974), and in Britain, Anderson (1977) notes that, depending upon the criteria used, 3 to 27 percent of elderly people in the community suffer from brain failure. Townsend (1962) finds that many of the aged in British institutions who were said to be mentally impaired were in fact often quite normal and had been victims of an inadequate diagnosis; frequently, many had been labelled "senile." More recently, in Britain an attempt is being made to make an accurate diagnosis when mental impairment is found. It appears that at Scottsdale patients are more carefully diagnosed and physical problems (e.g., infections, dehydration, and malnutrition) that can cause reversible brain syndrome are treated.

In the United States, by contrast, although much research has been done on the proper diagnosing of brain impairment (e.g., Simon and Cahan 1963; Wang 1973; Butler 1977), these research findings are not being applied in nursing home care. Terms such as senility, senile, and chronic brain syndrome are commonly used at Pacific Manor. Such terms are archaic and stigmatizing, carrying with them the implication of a hopeless and irreversible condition. Anderson (1977) says: "In my view nothing is worse than the term 'chronic brain syndrome,' which hides a multitude of sins." Many organic brain disorders, if properly diagnosed and treated, are reversible. Reversible brain syndrome, also known as acute brain syndrome, can be caused by congestive heart failure, malnutrition, anemia, infections, dehydration, and cerebrovascular accidents.

In the absence of a proper diagnosis, it is difficult to measure the degree of mental impairment of the institutionalized aged. The Mental Status Questionnaire (MSQ) was used in both institutions as a means of detecting intellectual impairment (Kahn et al. 1960.) There are ten questions on the questionnaire, and if the patient answers all of them correctly, he receives a score of ten. At Pacific Manor I found on several occasions that patients who were diagnosed as having chronic brain syndrome appeared quite normal. The MSQ bore out my preliminary judgment. Mrs. Crawford, a 93-year-old woman with congestive heart failure and chronic urinary tract infections also had a diagnosis of chronic brain syndrome. I administered the MSQ to her and she scored 9/10. Mrs. Crawford cannot read because of poor vision, but she keeps abreast of world affairs by listening to her radio every day. Not only does she keep informed of current news and politics, but she also has an opinion on timely issues such as the Panama Canal Treaty and the care of old people in the United States. One day she said, "I think the governor should walk through some of these places." "What do you think he would say?" I asked. "I think he would think this is a pretty bad way to treat the old people," she replied. "I think we should have national health insurance. It is terrible, between the doctors and hospitals, they have taken all of the old people's life savings," she remarked. These are hardly the statements of a mentally impaired woman.

A serious danger of improper diagnosis is that the nursing staff will adopt the judgment made by the physician, treat the elderly as if they are "senile," and fail to interact with them in a normal, adult manner. As a consequence, disorders that could be improved are worsened, and those patients who are normal can begin to deteriorate mentally.

Physical Illness

All patients at both institutions have an organic physical disease; however, the reliability of the data regarding patients' diagnoses is questionable. The problem of reliability arises because of the episodic, chronic, and cumulative multiple pathologies one frequently finds in the elderly. For instance, an elderly patient may have one illness, such as congestive heart failure, that is the predominant cause of his disability, while another (such as pneumonia) may have occurred after admission; additionally, he may have a chronic but still clinically significant condition such as diabetes mellitus. Finally, there may be some pathology, such as diverticulitis or cholecystitis, that is not at present causing significant clinical problems. The patients' medical records do not always reflect their current medical status. With all this in mind, the following data describe, as accurately as possible, the organic physical diseases in the two groups of institutionalized patients.

There is little difference in the mean number of diseases per patient at Scottsdale and Pacific Manor; 3.2 in the former group, 3.5 in the latter. Diseases of the circulatory system and rheumatoid arthritis are the leading causes of physical disability in both groups. Multiple sclerosis at Scottsdale and hip fractures at Pacific Manor are the next most predominant problem; these conditions along with diseases of the circulatory system and rheumatoid arthritis account for 92 percent of the physical problems at Scottsdale and 86 percent at Pacific Manor (see Table 6).

Admissions, Length of Institutionalization, Discharges, Deaths

The patient population at Scottsdale is much more stable than that at Pacific Manor. During calendar year 1976, at Scottsdale there were 52 admissions, 22 transfers and discharges, and 26 deaths. During calendar year 1977, at Pacific Manor, a slightly smaller facility, there were 111 admissions, 64 transfers and discharges, and 18 deaths. Clearly, there is a much larger turnover of patients at Pacific Manor; there were more than twice as many admissions and three times as many transfers in one year.

The large number of admissions may owe to the fact that in the United States Medicare will pay for no more than ninety days of inpatient hospital care during one hospital admission. Because of the very limited home health care services in the United States, patients who need nursing care following a hospitalization have as their only alternative admission to a nursing home. Thus a continual flow of patients from acute care hospitals to nursing homes results. By comparison, in Scotland, there is an extensive home health care program; many disabled elderly are cared for at home—only the severely disabled are admitted to long-term institutions.

The large number of transfers at Pacific Manor also needs to be explained. At Scottsdale of the twenty-two patients who were transferred or discharged, one went home, three went to continuing care units in neighboring communities, and eighteen were either readmitted to the geriatric assessment and rehabilitation unit or to acute units of a general hospital for medical or surgical care. Although the records at Pacific Manor are not precise, and thus difficult to interpret, it became apparent that a transfer and/or discharge may mean one of several things. A patient transfer at Pacific Manor may indicate: transfer to another nursing home, to a board and care home, to an acute-care hospital, or discharge to the patient's home. Upon inquiring of the staff, I learned that the majority of discharges and transfers actually represent readmission to an acute-care hospital.

During the course of my field work at Pacific Manor, I observed that on several occasions when patients became terminal, they were transferred to an acute-care hospital; one of the nurses said this was a common practice. Many of these patients die shortly after transfer from the nursing home. Thus the number of transfers may conceal the true number of deaths. During my three months at Scottsdale, only one patient from the original patient population died, as compared to thirteen from the original patient population during my four months at Pacific Manor; and of those thirteen, only two died in the nursing home. The remaining eleven were transferred to acute-care hospitals where they died shortly after admission.

The rapid turnover of patients at Pacific Manor brought about by the high rate of admissions and transfers accounts for the great difference in the average length of stay for patients in the two institutions. At Scottsdale the average length of time patients had been in the institution was 6 years (2 years, 6 months for male patients, and 7 years for female patients). By contrast, at Pacific Manor the average length of stay in the nursing home was 1 year 9 months (1 year 10 months for male patients and 1 year 8 months for female patients).

Payment for Care

As mentioned in Chapter 1, in Britain the National Health Service (NHS) pays for virtually every aspect of medical care, not only for the elderly but for all of the British people. Thus patients are admitted to Scottsdale irrespective of their financial status; the NHS pays for the entire cost of institutional care, in 1977 approximately £440 per month (about $840). If a patient's only income is a government pension, the pension, minus £3.05 per week, goes toward the cost of his care. The law stipulates that each person be allowed to keep that amount for personal use (the average rate of exchange in 1977 was $1.90 per pound sterling).

At Pacific Manor methods of payment vary according to the financial status of the patient: about 50 percent are privately supported patients, and 50 percent are on Medicare and Medicaid. The owner of the institution believes that he must maintain this 50:50 ratio to make a small profit. The cost for a privately supported patient is $1,100 to $1,200 per month, which covers only room and board; additional costs must be paid for pharmacy, medical supplies, physiotherapy, and speech therapy.

Medicare, a federally financed medical care program for the elderly, pays for care in a nursing home if the facility is staffed to provide skilled nursing care and rehabilitative services, and if it meets specified health, safety, and professional standards. It also helps pay for covered services in a skilled nursing facility if the following five conditions are met: (1) the patient must have been in the hospital for at least three consecutive days, not counting the day of discharge; (2) the patient must require further care for a condition treated in the hospital; (3) the patient must be admitted to the nursing home within fourteen days after discharge from the hospital; (4) the physician must certify that the patient needs either skilled nursing care or skilled rehabilitation (i.e., physiotherapy or speech therapy) on a daily basis (skilled nursing care is defined as care that must be given by a licensed nurse, that is, a registered nurse or a licensed practical nurse); (5) the patient's admission must be approved by the facility's Utilization Review Committee. When a patient meets these five conditions, Medicare will fully cover the first twenty days of care; after the first twenty days, the patient pays $18.00 a day for the next eighty days and Medicare pays the remainder. Following this one-hundred-day period, the patient either becomes a privately supported patient or, if he is not able to pay for his care, he is transferred to Medicaid (the state funded medical care program for the indigent).

Medicaid programs differ from state to state. To qualify for Medicaid, a person at Pacific Manor can have no more than $1,500 in cash (an additional $1,000 can be placed in an irrevocable trust to cover the cost of funeral arrangements). Thus if an elderly person had $5,000, he would have to deplete his cash resources before he would qualify for Medicaid. Because of this policy, many of the institutionalized elderly must become indigent before qualifying for financial support for long-term care. Most of the patients who are currently on Medicaid at Pacific Manor had previously been privately financed patients; over the months and years of institutionalization, they have exhausted all of their personal funds. The cost of long-term care is a burden even for those with considerable means, and it is a matter that causes stress, anxiety, and concern for both patients and their families.

The patients at Pacific Manor are older, have a greater prevalence of mental impairment, and display a wider range of physical and mental disability. Moreover, there is a much greater turnover of patients in the American nursing home. The mortality rate is also much higher among patients at Pacific Manor. Because of the greater turnover of patients and the wide range of their disabilities, Pacific Manor appears to be a combination of a chronic, long-term-care institution and a semi-acute-care institution; it has the appearance and feeling of an acute-care hospital. By contrast, there is much less patient turnover at Scottsdale, the physical environment is more homelike, and there is more of a feeling of community and camaraderie among staff and patients.

Despite these differences, there are many similarities between the residents of the two institutions; they are largely white, single or widowed women over 70 years of age, and most have living relatives. In both institutions there are patients with multiple physical disabilities and mental impairment.

Two differences that perhaps are significant—length of institutionalization and method of payment for care—merit a brief discussion. At Scottsdale, the average length of time patients had been in the institution was 6 years, while at Pacific Manor it was 1 year 9 months. It could be argued that at Scottsdale, because of the longer average stay, social bonds develop between the aged and their caretakers, and that these bonds account for a higher level of care. But one might also propose that patients who are institutionalized for long periods become inflexible and demanding and that this could contribute to difficulties in patient-staff relationships and, subsequently, lower levels of care. The staff at Pacific Manor remarked that they preferred to have a constant turnover of patients; new admissions added variety to their work and made it more interesting and less depressing, they said.

Payment for care is significant in that at Scottsdale neither staff nor patients ever mentioned the cost of care, whereas at Pacific Manor it was a constant source of concern to both the patients and staff. At Scottsdale it was accepted that the elderly were entitled to care paid for by the government; and the personnel, too, received health care paid for by the National Health Service. At Pacific Manor some patients were paying privately for care, while others were publicly supported patients. The administrative staff clearly prefer the privately funded patients; they are essential for making a profit for the owner, a constant concern of both the administrative and nursing personnel. I did not attempt to evaluate if privately funded patients received a higher level of care than publicly supported patients. Many other variables, such as frequency of visitors, level of physical and mental impairment, and even the personality of the patient, are involved. However, I did observe that on some occasions (see Chapter 8) patients with resources were able to request services in exchange for money or goods. Hence, I believe that the potential for differential and preferential treatment is greater in an institution that has a combination of privately and publicly financed patients. The above-mentioned features may, in part, account for some of the difference in the level of care, but they are not wholly responsible.

6

The Care of the Institutionalized Aged

The preceding chapter described the medical disorders and functional disabilities of the institutionalized aged. To deal successfully with the multiple medical and social problems of the aged in long-term-care facilities, an extensive staff of professional and nonprofessional health workers is needed. Central to this staff are the doctors and nurses who must provide the professional knowledge, skills, and leadership to ameliorate the multiple pathologies, as well as the social, cultural, and psychological problems of late life. Doctors are essential to provide prompt medical care and continuous medical observation, and professional and nonprofessional nursing staff must provide care on a twenty-four-hour basis. Hence, the quality of the care of patients is largely determined by the manner in which doctors and nurses fulfill their professional roles.

Medical care for the institutionalized aged in Scotland and the United States differs primarily because of the organization and financing of health care services. In Britain, physicians are divided into two groups: general practitioners and consultants (i.e., specialists). The general practitioner is a primary-care physician and does not provide medical care to hospitalized patients. The "consultants," who provide all medical care in hospitals, are salaried employees; salaries are set by the government and are standard throughout the country (see Chapter 7).

69

Of the 71,000 active physicians in Britain in 1973, approximately 35 percent were in general practice, 50 percent were in full-time or part-time hospital work, and the remainder in universities, industry, the military, or public health work. The number of consultants is limited by the number of posts available at the major hospitals; 17 percent of all physicians are specialists at the consultant level (Committee on Ways and Means 1976).

Of the 301,000 active physicians in the United States in 1974, 82 percent were practicing in one or more speciality areas, and 18 percent were in general practice; both groups have hospital privileges (Committee on Ways and Means 1976). Although some physicians in the United States are employed by governmental agencies and prepaid group plans such as the Kaiser-Permanente Foundation in California, the prevailing American medical system is based on solo or group fee-for-service practice. Physicians operate as private entrepreneurs and charge each patient a fee for services rendered. Even with Medicare, physicians charge for services at their usual, customary, and prevailing fees, giving them, rather than the government, the right to establish charges.

Medical Care at Scottsdale

At Scottsdale three specialists in geriatric medicine ("geriatricians") and one house physician provide medical care for all patients. Since the hospital consultant is a salaried employee, there is no charge to the patient for the care he provides. The chief geriatrician is ultimately responsible for the care of all patients at Scottsdale, sharing this responsibility with his two junior colleagues and other medical staff. Each of the three geriatricians provides medical care on a continuous basis for about one-third of the patients (i.e., about thirty-two each) and visits them weekly. This continuity of care is an outstanding feature of the medical care at Scottsdale. Since, as mentioned earlier, every patient is admitted from the geriatric assessment and rehabilitation unit, the geriatrician who has cared for him during the period of assessment and rehabilitation continues to see him throughout his stay at Scottsdale.

In addition to the geriatrician's weekly visits, patients are seen daily by the house physician, a general practitioner on duty from 8 A.M. to 12 P.M. Monday through Friday. Although she does not visit every patient individually, she makes rounds daily, consults with the nurse in charge, and personally visits any patient who needs medical attention. If a problem not within her expertise arises, she contacts the attending geriatrician. Even on weekends and holidays the hospital is not without medical coverage. Each weekend one of the geriatricians makes rounds; additionally, because Scottsdale is part of the geriatric service of a general hospital, the physician on call at the geriatric unit of the hospital is also on call for any medical emergency that may occur. "The doctors are very good about coming when we call," remarked one of the nurses.

At Scottsdale the patients, as well as the nursing staff, spoke highly of the chief geriatrician, commented on how hard he had worked to promote geriatric care in the region, and knew that if any problem regarding medical care for a patient should arise, they could turn to him for assistance. There was great respect for him, and the nurses endeavored to have their ward in order on the day they expected him for rounds. Frequently he dropped by at unexpected times, and it was quite obvious that his presence and concern had a positive influence on the continuing care of patients at Scottsdale.

Medical Care at Pacific Manor

At Pacific Manor each patient is cared for by a private physician, and each doctor charges a fee for his service. However, as we have seen, this does not mean all patients are responsible for all of their expenses. Medical care for most is paid, at least in part, by Medicare Part B or Medicaid. Medicare Part B, a medical insurance program for which the aged pay a monthly fee of $8.90, does not provide comprehensive coverage for all medical services. It will pay 80 percent of reasonable charges for covered services provided by physicians. Doctors' services not covered by medical insurance include routine physical examinations, routine foot care, and eye or hearing examinations.

There is a great difference in the amount of medical care patients receive at the two institutions. Patients at Pacific Manor are usually visited only once a month by their private physician. The original Medicare and Medicaid policy required physicians to visit nursing home patients every thirty days. But in 1974 new and less stringent regulations were announced that required doctors to visit patients every thirty days for the first ninety days and at sixty-day intervals thereafter (Moss and Halamandaris 1977). At Pacific Manor, however, state law requires the physician to see a patient within 48 hours of admission and to make monthly visits thereafter. Some physicians at Pacific Manor are very conscientious and not only make the required monthly visits, but come weekly or even daily if the patient's condition warrants more frequent care. For example, Mrs. O'Sullivan, a patient for 8 years with no living relatives in the area, remarked that her physician had never missed a monthly visit. Moreover, every Christmas he bring her a poinsettia, and on some occasions he has brought his children along to visit her.

Not all physicians are as faithful as this. Indeed, many patients express concern because their doctor has not visited them for several months; many feel rejected and neglected because of infrequent visits. "I called my doctor last week and he still hasn't come," complained Mrs. Tyler. "He used to come when I called, but he doesn't any more; I am going to have to get another doctor." Mrs. Crawford, a patient for 4–½ years who has exhausted her financial resources, said: "Some months last year my doctor didn't come at all. I told him when he came that he was falling down on the job. I don't know why he doesn't come; I always paid him every cent I owed him, but now I think he doesn't come because he doesn't get enough money because I am on Medicaid."

In cases of a physician's neglect, the responsibility for contacting the doctor falls upon the nursing staff. Some nurses repeatedly call a physician reminding him that he has not made the regular visit. In many cases, however, unless it is a medical crisis, the nurse calls the doctor, makes a notation of the call in the nurses' notes, and does not pursue the matter further. Once the call has been made and documented, the nurse's responsibility to the state requirement has been fulfilled. Failure of the doctor to make the required visit to his patient will not in any way jeopardize the nursing home. "Does the state cite the doctor for failure to provide medical care?" I asked. "No one goes after the doctor," replied the director of nursing. The regulation that patients be visited monthly appears never to have been enforced in the United States, as disclosed by a 1971 audit in three states that revealed that the regulation was violated in more than 50 percent of the homes surveyed (Moss and Halamandaris 1977).

Patients' Evaluation of the Physicians' Care

In both Scotland and the United States, the doctor is seen by patients as the person most responsible for medical care. Thus, to assess satisfaction or dissatisfaction with their care, patients in each institution were asked

"How do you find your doctor?" If patients had difficulty interpreting this question, it was rephrased: "How do you feel about your medical care?" and the responses were ranked on a scale of 1 to 5, as described in Chapter 3. At Scottsdale the mean was found to be 4.5 (i.e., a very high degree of satisfaction): 80 percent of the respondents gave replies that indicated they were completely satisfied with their medical care, 16 percent gave an intermediate response that indicated satisfaction but not strong enthusiasm for their care, and only one patient out of twenty-five interviewed expressed some degree of dissatisfaction with medical care. This patient elaborated: "They don't bother with you as much as they should, but I would feel free to talk to them if I had any problem."

At Scottsdale typical responses to the question "How do you find the doctors?" were quite positive:

"I like them very much."

"We have a lady doctor who comes every day and she is very nice."

"Oh, the doctors are good here; they're all good."

"My doctor is very, very nice. He usually comes twice a week."

"Oh, well, they are all very good, but there is one special one whom I like very much—that is Dr. Ross. He's done a lot for me."

"Dr. Hall, the lady doctor, comes every forenoon, and if she doesn't come another doctor comes."

"Dr. Ross is very good. He's my consultant doctor, and he usually comes twice a week."

Obviously, patients at Scottsdale are remarkably satisfied with their medical care, they feel confidence in their physician, and they know that if they need a doctor, one is always available.

At Pacific Manor, by contrast, the patients' responses to the same question indicate much dissatisfaction and concern about the lack of medical care. A mean of only 2.0 was obtained: 80 percent of the patients indicated dissatisfaction with their medical care, 15 percent gave an intermediate response that suggested some satisfaction with their care, and only one patient reported complete satisfaction with her medical care. This patient said of her doctor: "He is a very nice, kind man. He comes once a month; then if I need something he puts it on the chart." At Pacific Manor typical responses to the question "How do you find your doctor?" ranged from neutral to negative:

> "He sees me once a month. That is common, I understand, for these kinds of places."

> "He doesn't come often; he calls up once in a while."

> "I am going to change doctors. He usually comes when I call him, but once I called him on Monday and he didn't come until Saturday. When I had the flu, he didn't come at all; he told them to give me penicillin, and I am allergic to penicillin."

> "They are supposed to come once a month, but sometimes he skips. I don't think he likes to come here. Maybe the state doesn't pay them enough."

> "He comes about once a month and just takes my blood pressure and listens to my heart and lungs. He stays about 10 minutes, and then I don't see him for another month."

> "He comes here, not to see me but stops on his way to another hospital. He passes the door and then stops to see me. The doctor is an awfully nice man, but I very seldom see him— maybe once a month—I never get very much attention."

> "I told the doctor about my eyes, and he said: 'There is nothing wrong with your eyes.' They pay no attention to you. I fell down twice."

Many of the patients' responses on the questionnaire expressed concern with lack of attention to medical needs, yet patients seemed to realize they were entitled to only one visit per month from the physician. The limitation of one visit per month produced concern, anxiety, and fear in the elderly, who felt they needed more frequent medical attention. It also made it difficult for the nursing staff to call the physician and request additional visits.

This problem is poignantly illustrated in the case of Mrs. Lester, a 73-year-old woman who looked much younger than her years, despite the fact that she had lost all her hair because of radiation therapy. First admitted to a hospital for diagnosis (cancer of the lung with metastasis to the brain), she was then transferred to a second hospital for radiation therapy, after which she was admitted to Pacific Manor. The social worker in the acute-care hospital had noted on the chart, "Patient is very frightened and overwhelmed by her illness and treatment, but is coping o.k."

A nurse at Pacific Manor explained to me that because Mrs. Lester was a Christian Scientist she had not sought medical care until her disease was far advanced. When she did seek medical care, her Christian Science practitioner became angry and "washed his hands of her," and since she had been admitted to the nursing home her doctors had not visited her. Hence, she was feeling rejected both by her church and her physician. She was also separated from her husband and had no children. "That's what makes it hard," she observed. She had one sister-in-law and three cousins who lived in the city.

Since Mrs. Lester's admission to the nursing home on 12 January 1978, the nurse had repeatedly called the doctor's office asking that he come to see her; however, although the law says he must visit within 48 hours after admission, he did not come until 19 January 1978.

Two weeks later, on 3 February 1978, I was at the nurse's desk when a visitor came and asked if the nurse would call the doctor and ask him to see Mrs. Lester. I went to see Mrs. Lester again and was surprised to see how quickly her condition had deteriorated; she no longer responded verbally and appeared to be in the terminal phase of her illness. The visitor, a cousin by marriage, was very distressed because the doctor had seen Mrs. Lester only once. In the presence of the visitor, the nurse in charge called the doctor, explained that the family was concerned, and described the patient's condition. The doctor replied that he only had to visit once a month. The nurse said she understood, but she explained that when patients are terminal the staff try to get the doctor out a bit more frequently. The relative then asked if she could speak with the doctor; to her request for a visit, he replied, "I just don't have time; do you know it is five miles for me to come out there?" He said it would be four to five days before he would be able to come. Further, he told the nurse that if the family members were not satisfied they could get another physician.

Both the nurse and the patient's relative were greatly upset by the doctor's attitude. Later the nurse said: "We know there is nothing he can do medically; all we are asking for is a little humanitarianism, but he has none to give. I get this all the time with doctors who have patients in the nursing home; they admit them and just write them off." The doctor finally visited Mrs. Lester on 7 February 1978, and one day later, when I arrived at the nursing home, the nurse told me she had died the night before. "At least the doctor came before she died," she observed with resignation. I didn't think she would go so fast, but I am glad she did; she was so depressed. She just gave up."

Other staff and patients made similar statements that suggest patients at Pacific Manor feel—and probably are—neglected and rejected by their physicians. The nurse in charge of Unit B said that, on some occasions when she had suggested glasses or a hearing aid for a patient, the doctor had rejected this suggestion with, "Oh well, she's old anyhow." Mr. Franklin, a patient, said, "There are too many patients here whom the doctors have rejected or turned away." A young woman who came to the nursing home periodically to do speech therapy put it succinctly: "I would rather work in an acute-care hospital because the patients in nursing homes are the ones doctors have given up on." She had been giving speech therapy for one week to an aphasic patient and wanted to continue, but the doctor did not want her to. The therapist went on, "I even went to the trouble of going all the way to his office to ask him if I could continue for one more month; he finally agreed to a one-month trial period." "Won't Medicare pay for it?" I asked. She replied, "Yes, that's what I told the doctor, but he said, 'Yes, but that's my tax dollar that is paying for it!'" At this time the month's trial period was nearly over. Although the patient had shown some progress, the therapist later reported the doctor would not authorize her to continue therapy.

On one occasion a physician admitted an elderly woman to the nursing home and then refused to care for her. Eighty-nine-year-old Mrs. Edwards had been in an acute-care hospital with a fractured hip. Her doctor told her that she must leave the hospital and go to the nursing home. "When he told me I had to leave the hospital, he said he would come here to see me," she explained. "He told me a lot of things to get me out of the hospital. He was my doctor for 15 years; now they say he has released me to a new doctor, and I don't even know the new doctor." When Mrs. Edwards's physician refused to care for her in the nursing home, the nursing staff called a doctor who frequently has patients at the nursing home and he agreed to be her attending physician. Thinking there must be some misunderstanding, I approached her newly acquired doctor and asked what had happened to Mrs. Edwards's personal physician. "He just abandoned her," he said.

There is a wide variation both in the quantity and quality of medical care in the two institutions. During the course of the research at Scottsdale, the adequacy of medical care was never a subject for discussion. Indeed, it was simply understood that patients would receive whatever medical care was necessary, whereas at Pacific Manor the lack of medical care and concern for medical needs was frequently a subject for discussion both with patients and the nursing staff. Inattention to patients' needs at Pacific Manor causes anxiety, stress, and fear among the patients and creates frustration among the nursing staff, who are helpless to improve the situation. When a problem involving medical care does arise, there is no one to whom they can turn for help. There is no formal organization or structure to ensure adequate medical care for the institutionalized aged at Pacific Manor.

Patients' Evaluation of Nursing Care

Although doctors are essential for diagnosing and treating the institutionalized aged, it is the nursing staff who must provide care on a 24-hour basis. Consequently, in some respects the quality of care for the aged depends more upon the quality of the nursing care than upon any other single factor. Many of the problems associated with the chronic illnesses and functional disabilities of old age can be dealt with successfully by a competent nursing staff. Thus the importance of properly qualified nursing personnel cannot be overemphasized; it is a role that is essential to the care and well-being of every institutionalized elderly person.

Before beginning the discussion of nursing at Scottsdale, I must define some terms. In 1970 a reorganization of nursing took place in Scotland, and a new plan, called the "Salmon Scheme," was introduced. With this reorganization, nurses at various levels of leadership received new titles. For example, at the top level the title of matron was changed to "nursing officer" (grade 8); below her is a "nursing officer" (grade 7); and the lowest level administrator (formerly called "sister") is now referred to as "charge nurse" (grade 6). But because this new terminology is somewhat confusing, I will use the old terms. Accordingly, a matron in Scotland is equivalent to a director of nursing, an assistant matron has duties similar to those of an assistant director of nursing, and a sister has a role akin to that of a head nurse or charge nurse in the United States.

In both institutions, patients were asked "How do you find the nurses?" and responses were ranked on a scale of 1 to 5. At Scottsdale the mean for the question was 4.5: 88 percent of the respondents expressed complete satisfaction with their nursing care; 12 percent, partial satisfaction; and none complete dissatisfaction.

At Pacific Manor the mean response was 3.25: only 35 percent of the patients interviewed expressed complete satisfaction with their care, while 40 percent expressed partial satisfaction, and 25 percent complete dissatisfaction. Six of the twenty patients at Pacific Manor were completely satisfied with their care and replied accordingly:

> "The nurses are very nice; they have a nice attitude."

> "Fine, I like it here. I always tell them they are so good to me, and they say 'why shouldn't we be?' "

> "The girls are very nice and understanding."

> "The head nurse is just a darling; she is great!"

Four were completely dissatisfied with care at Pacific Manor:

> "I hardly see them; they hardly pay any attention to me."

> "They don't like me. If I ask them a question, they won't answer me. They go by the door, but they never stop in to see me."

> "I can't move unless they move me, and I never know when they will get angry at me. When I get wet, they say 'You just lay in it,' or 'I will come back pretty soon.' "

> "There are all kinds; we have nurses here that it is really a crime, really a disgrace to have them come into your room and talk to patients the way they do, and of course the only thing we can do is say nothing. Sometimes the nurse grabs the bedside curtain and closes it and says 'You shut your big mouth,'

and they keep the curtain closed just to be mean to you, and there is nothing to do because the less you say the better. This one woman is mean, disrespectful; the only thing I can do is be quiet. But the charge nurse is a perfect lady."

There were significantly more patients at Scottsdale who were completely satisfied with their nursing care. Fifteen of the twenty-five interviewed gave responses that indicated complete satisfaction with their nursing care, for instance:

"We couldn't get a better group of girls anywhere. I really mean that; they are all very kind, very nice.-'

"They are very kind. When I have accidents, they don't make a fuss. They say, "Don't think about it.' If you sneeze sometimes you have an accident, and I feel so ashamed."

"They are awfully good, so understanding—especially the auxiliaries."

"They really are most kind; they are very thoughtful."

Apparent throughout the responses at Scottsdale were such words as *kind, thoughtful,* and *understanding.* The patients especially seemed to value the nurse who was kind to them even under adverse circumstances, such as wetting the bed. "They don't treat me as if I were a baby," remarked one woman.

Overall, the questionnaire revealed more complete satisfaction with nursing care at Scottsdale than at Pacific Manor. This disparity is apparently due to differences in staffing and salaries of nurses at the two institutions.

Staffing

It is difficult to make exact comparisons in regard to staffing at the two institutions. Both facilities employ a large number of part-time employees—40 percent at Pacific Manor and 47 percent at Scottsdale—and there is wide variation as to how many hours a week the part-time employee may work. The following discussion of staffing, therefore, will present a gross quantitative comparison supplemented by some qualitative data.

At Scottsdale a matron is in charge of the nursing staff, with full responsibility for the nursing care of the ninety-six patients; she also has administrative duties at two other hospitals. Under the supervision of the matron is an assistant matron and sisters who are responsible for each of the wards. Lower level staff-nurses (registered nurses), enrolled nurses (nurses who have completed a two-year training program), and nursing auxiliaries make up the remainder of the staff.

At Pacific Manor there is a director of nursing service (she has no assistant) and a charge nurse (a registered nurse or licensed vocational nurse) for each of the two units. It must be remembered, however, that the units are much larger at Pacific Manor, 44–45 beds each as compared to 18–27-bed units at Scottsdale. Pacific Manor also employs licensed vocational nurses (LVNs) and nurse aides. State law requires that for a facility of 60 beds or more, in addition to the director of nursing service, there must be at least one registered nurse or LVN on duty at all times.

At Scottsdale there is clearly more professional staff on duty; typically, on a given day there are four charge sisters plus the matron and assistant matron, while at Pacific Manor there are only two registered nurses in addition to the director of nursing service. At Scottsdale there is a total of eighty-one nursing staff (forty-three full-time and thirty-eight part-time) for ninety-six patients compared to fifty-four nursing staff (thirty-two full-time and twenty-two part-time) for eighty-five patients at Pacific Manor.

Length of Employment

The nursing staff at both institutions is relatively stable; 66 percent at Pacific Manor and 79 percent at Scottsdale have been employed for more than a year. Table 7 shows the length of employment of nursing staff in both institutions.

Although gross figures are quite similar, for those in nursing administration and head nurse positions at the two institutions, there is less stability at Pacific Manor than at Scottsdale. For example, the current

Table 7. Length of employment of nursing staff (in percentage)

	Less than 1 year	1–5 years	6–10 years	11 years and over
Pacific Manor	34	34	26	6
Scottsdale	21	48	27	4

director of nursing at Pacific Manor has been there for less than a year, and in the past 11 years there have been six nurses in that position. (One head nurse, however, has been there for 5 years.) By comparison, the matron at Scottsdale has been in her position for 7 years, and the assistant matron for 11 years. One sister has been employed at Scottsdale for 8 years; the remaining three sisters have been there for 2 to 3 years.

Stability of staff is important at both the professional and nonprofessional levels. The nurse aides provide day-to-day bedside care to the patients, and patients feel secure with those who have come to know them, understand their special needs, and provide care for them in an orderly, organized fashion. "I just love my nurse," beamed Mrs. Crawford (a patient at Pacific Manor for 4½ years). "When she's on duty, she does everything right, but I only have her every third week. But even if she doesn't take care of me, she comes to see me and if she doesn't I ask for her; she comes in every day. If I have something bothering me, I tell Mrs. Lee." Mrs. Lee is a 55-year-old nurse aide who has been employed at Pacific Manor throughout that time; it is clear that an excellent relationship has developed between these two women. This example illustrates the importance of enduring relationships between auxiliary staff and patients. But stability of staff at the administrative level is also extremely important. Those in nursing administration and head nurse positions provide the professional leadership and determine in large part the quality of nursing care. Lack of stability in these positions inevitably leads to a lack of organization of care and lack of direction for the auxiliary staff.

Unit B at Pacific Manor has a fairly stable staff; the head nurse, as noted, has been there for 5 years, and she is very competent and dependable. Still, the director of nursing service has been trying for months to staff Unit A with a charge nurse on the day (7 A.M. to 3:30 P.M.) and evening (3 P.M. to 11 P.M.) shifts. During one week, there was a different nurse in charge each day, and one of the patients said there had been a different charge nurse every evening. "They don't know what to do," mused Mr. Franklin (a patient). "You have to tell them where things are and what to do." He had been watching the medication cart for over an hour on this particular evening while the nurse in charge had gone off to dinner leaving it unattended. Mr. Franklin was fearful that a confused patient might be harmed by drinking some of the large bottles of antiseptics that were on the cart.

The nurse aides on Unit A are the only permanent staff on the ward, and those who have been employed at the nursing home for 10 to 15 years have become a strongly entrenched group that sets its own standards and makes its own rules. "I'm not coming to work tomorrow, " announced Mrs. Moore one day; "I'm tired." "I'm not coming either," added Mrs. Lee. The charge nurse and the director of nursing service were not consulted; they were not even told. The two nurse aides simply did not report for work the following day.

In Chapter 2 it was noted that few patients ever make use of the pleasant patio area. I asked one of the charge nurses about this and she answered: "The only ones who get out on the patio are those who have relatives who come and push them out there. You will never see any of the staff take them out. They think that if they give them a bath, get them up in the chair, and push them into the lounge that is enough; they would never think of doing anything extra." On one occasion this nurse personally took some of the patients to the patio. It was a lovely, sunny day; so when the lunch trays arrived, she suggested the aides serve them lunch on the patio. "What a row there was," she remarked. The nurse aides complained very loudly because they would have to carry the lunch trays to the patients in the courtyard. "Some of the staff have been here so long and are so set in their ways," she charged, "they don't like any change and no one can tell them what to do, not even the director of nursing service or the administrator."

Staffing is a problem at both Scottsdale and Pacific Manor, and nurses in both institutions feel this is partly so because geriatrics is not a popular specialty. In Scotland several nurses said that geriatrics has been the "poor relation" for many years. Similarly, in the United States there is an unwillingness or reluctance on the part of registered nurses and nursing students to work with geriatric patients in general hospitals and nursing homes (Gunter 1971; Campbell 1971; Kayser and Minnigerode 1975).

Yet the staff shortage at Scottsdale appears to be related more to cuts in the budget for health care than to an inability to hire nursing staff. Britain has experienced a high rate of inflation in recent years; since 1974 shortage of staff in hospitals has become a chronic problem because of the financial pinch. Even in some of the large general hospitals, wards have been shut down due to lack of funds for staff.

In recent years the staff at Scottsdale has been cut by 10 percent, and nearly every week complaints were raised by the personnel about the lack of help. Nursing staff complain that they do not have time to sit and talk with patients; "that's an important part of geriatric nursing," declared nurse Markson, "but we never have time to do it." The shortage of personnel has led to low morale among even the most dedicated workers, clearly the most serious problem among the nursing staff at Scottsdale. Scottsdale has been known as a model institution, it has developed a fine reputation over the years, and the nurses are bitter about the cuts in staffing. Many of the patients are immobile, need to be fed, and are very dependent on the nurses for care. When they are short-staffed, only the basic care can be given. "We used to have time to take patients for walks around the garden, but we don't have the staff to do it any more," said one of the sisters. "When we are short-staffed something has to give, and sometimes it means that patients' backs begin to break down from lack of care." Working with geriatric patients is very demanding and challenging. It is difficult for nurses to cope with any added stress.

Conversely, the staffing problems at Pacific Manor are caused by multiple factors. First and foremost is the poor image of nursing homes. To be associated with a nursing home is to suggest a lack of competence on the part of a nurse, and in the United States to work in an institution for the aged is to occupy a low-status positon.

Consequently, many nurses, even if they would enjoy geriatric care, refuse to accept a position in a nursing home. To add to the problem, working conditions are very poor in most nursing homes; salaries are low and fringe benefits are few. At Pacific Manor a nurse aide earns about $2.65 per hour, whereas the beginning hourly salary for a nurse aide in an acute-care hospital is $5.80; interestingly, both employees belong to the same union. Salaries for licensed personnel are also low. A licensed vocational nurse at Pacific Manor is hired at $4.25 per hour, whereas at an acute-care hospital a licensed vocational nurse begins at $6.00 per hour. And a registered nurse at Pacific Manor earns a starting salary of only $6.00 per hour, or approximately $960.00 a month; her contemporary in an acute-care hospital in the same city earns $1,270.00 per month.

Low salaries obviously add greatly to the problem of recruitment of nursing staff. The director of nursing staff said she cannot compete for competent staff, and the administrator agreed: "You get two kinds of people, those who really like geriatrics and are willing to work at a lower salary, and those who can't work anywhere else." Unfortunately, more of the latter frequently are found in nursing homes.

I walked into the lounge one day and saw an elderly woman in a white uniform walking about with medications and calling: "Mrs. Thomas, who is Mrs. Thomas? Can anyone help me find Mrs. Thomas?" There was no response from the other patients. She then began to call for Mr. Sampson: "I am looking for Mr. Sampson." One of the patients stopped reading her newspaper, pointed to a patient, and said, "That is Mr. Sampson." The nurse giving the medications began again to call for Mrs. Thomas. Another patient said, "There are two Mrs. Thomases; there's one of them." This nurse was still distributing 9 A.M. medications at 2 P.M. I do not know when she dispensed the medications that were to be given at 1 P.M. One of the staff said that this particular nurse had been on duty over the weekend and was so disorganized that none of the treatments had been done for the patients for three days. "It does little good for us to do treatments and give patients back care when it isn't maintained over the weekend," he pointed out. "That's why I am quitting."

In addition to attracting the incompetent nurse, nursing homes in cities in which there is a large influx of foreign nurses also attract foreign nurses. Some of the foreign nurses are excellent practitioners and have a strong commitment to geriatric care; however, others look upon the job as merely a stepping stone to a position in an acute-care hospital. Foreign nurses must pass the state board examination and receive a license before they can be employed as registered nurses in an acute-care facility; in fact, many work in nursing homes only while preparing for this examination. "I am here to learn what nursing is like in the United States," said a young nurse from India, "and I don't want to get stuck in a nursing home." This young Indian nurse had been in the United States less than a year, but already she has learned that to "really be a nurse" one must work in an acute-care hospital.

Because salaries are low in nursing homes, it is not uncommon for staff members to have two positions. Some, by working a variety of shifts, are in fact able to hold down two full-time positions. I was standing at the nursing station one day at 12 noon when the young nurse mentioned above came into the nursing home. "Orient yourself," said the director of nursing service; "you're in charge tonight." The (male) nurse in charge on the day shift who was put in charge of orienting this new employee had been called to work through the nurses' registry and had never before worked at Pacific Manor. He attempted to explain some of the routines, procedures, and paperwork to her before he left at 3:30 P.M. I looked in disbelief at this young woman, who would be in charge of the care of forty-five patients that evening, and wondered how she could manage. It was even more unbelievable to arrive early the next morning and find this same nurse again on duty at 7 A.M. I asked her if she wasn't very tired from having worked nearly 12 hours the previous evening. "Oh, yes," she replied, "and I have to work until 11 P.M. tonight." She further told me that these two days were in fact her days off; she was working full-time at another facility. In a 36-hour period, this nurse worked 28 hours with only eight hours off for rest. The quality of nursing care one can give under such conditions is questionable indeed.

While low salaries are a constant source of discontent among the nursing staff at Pacific Manor and contribute greatly toward the problem of obtaining competent staff, at Scottsdale salaries are not an issue. Unlike their counterparts in the United States, British nursing staff who care for geriatric patients receive a salary identical to nurses in an acute-care facility. Nursing salaries are established by the government and are standard throughout the country: all nurses are paid the same regardless of their place of employment. Nurses who work in geriatrics and psychiatry, moreover, annually receive what is referred to as "lead pay." This is an annual bonus of approximately £165 (about $315). Although it is not a large pay differential, and some say the additional money does not serve as an incentive to work in geriatrics, several nurses noted that it was a factor in their decision to work at Scottsdale.

Bringing the salaries of staff in nursing homes in line with that of nursing personnel in other medical facilities would not solve all of the problems in nursing homes; but, clearly, in a society that values material wealth, it is impossible to expect a high quality of care when paying the lowest possible salaries.

The present-day standards of long-term care of the elderly have evolved out of the structure of the health care services in each country. It is important, then, to compare the historical development of health care services that has resulted in a comprehensive health service in Britain—and its subsequent geriatric service for the elderly—to the Medicare and Medicaid program—and the evolution of nursing home care for the elderly—in the United States.

7

Historical Development of Health Care Services

The problems of the elderly in Britain and the United States are similar; nevertheless, there are major differences in the approach to the care of the disabled elderly in the two countries.

Although the historical development of medical care in the two countries may be of interest and clearly does have some relevance in current governmental policy toward the care of the aged, it is a complex subject that lies without the scope of this book. I will make no attempt, therefore, to present a detailed picture of this historical development. Rather, because the structure of a medical care system is related to the social, economic, and ethical values of the society of which it is a part, I will briefly discuss the social conditions responsible for the development of public health policy and subsequent governmental programs for personal health care in each country. Additionally, some comparison will be made in an attempt to explain the differences in the present-day approach to the care of the aged.

Although the United States and Great Britain possess a common language, and the first American physicians were trained in Britain, our health care systems have developed in strikingly different ways. In Great Britain a welfare state has evolved, and within it, the National Health Service is the organ by which medical care is provided. The National Health Service, which came into being on 5 July 1948, pays for virtually the entire range of health and medical care without regard to age, income, need, or insurance qualification.

In the United States medical care is financed publicly by the federal, state, and local government and privately by health insurance companies and direct payments by patients to physicians on a fee-for-service basis. In the past the private share has always been by far the largest, but in recent years, because of the Medicare and Medicaid programs, there has been a shift to more public financing. With the 1965 enactment of Medicare for the aged and Medicaid for the poor, the government established the first major federally financed program that provides hospital and medical insurance protection both for people 65 years of age and older and for the indigent.

Historical Development of Health Care Services in Britain

Britain has a long social history, and provision of medical care and social services has evolved and adapted through changing sociological systems over the past 300 years. In the Middle Ages the benevolent landlord was responsible, if he so wished, for providing medical services for his tenants and servants; he also provided for his people in their infirmity, disability, and old age.

Infirmary almshouses and Houses of Pity for the destitute, sick, and aged were run largely by the monasteries. The medieval church took a positive approach to human distress by emphasizing that the relief of distress was as important for the giver as for the person in need. This doctrine lent dignity to poverty and made the granting of alms a meritorious deed. In the sixteenth century, Henry VIII expropriated the monasteries and turned over their properties to his followers. After this transition, hospitals became secular institutions and charitable bodies maintained the majority of hospitals for acute care. Voluntary hospitals began to be established in all parts of the country during the eighteenth century; and in the nineteenth century, there was a rapid growth of the voluntary hospital movement (Stevens 1966:14).

In the nineteenth century, personal health care was primarily regarded as the responsibility of the individual. The Poor Laws did make some provision for the care of the indigent who were ill; infirmaries were usually attached to the workhouses. Other groups organized among the poorer people to provide some sort of prepayment insurance; and by the end of the nineteenth century, there were large Friendly Societies providing, under contract, some type of medical care as well as payments during illness (U.S. Department of Health, Education and Welfare 1976).

In the same era concern for the environment arose. By the middle of the nineteenth century, government began to concern itself with improving sanitation, particularly in the cities, a concern brought about by the movement of masses of people during the Industrial Revolution. With the Industrial Revolution of the eighteenth and nineteenth centuries, England was among the first countries to be faced with urban slums, open sewers, and contaminated water supplies. From 1801 to 1851 the population of England grew from 8,892,000 to 17,927,000 (Brand 1965). Urban industrial life created major medical and social problems as cholera epidemics swept through England in 1831, 1848, and 1853. Chadwick's study (1842), "Report of an Inquiry into the Sanitary Conditions of the Labouring Population of Great Britain," described the sanitary ills of the nation and provided the impetus for much of the public health legislation that followed. This report led to the passing of the Public Health Act of 1848 (Brand 1965:3). The "sanitary idea," or Chadwick's principle—that improvement in the material environment would advance the physical wellbeing of the English people—was of far more importance to mid-nineteenth-century sanitation reformers than the improvement of public medical care (Brand 1965:3). Public measures to promote healthier living conditions, it seems, preceded adequate public provision for the care of the sick.

The extension of public medicine was a social rather than a scientific phenomenon and stemmed largely from the public health legislation of the late nineteenth and early twentieth centuries (Stevens 1966:36). Public health systems had been introduced throughout Europe; and following Bismarck's example in Germany, David Lloyd George, Chancellor of the Exchequer, introduced the National Health Insurance Act in 1911. This legislation provided a method whereby all people earning wages of less than £160 a year were entitled to the services of a general practitioner in return for their own regular contributions and those of their employers to certain insurance organizations known as approved societies; no provision was made for their dependents. The National Insurance Act of 1911 provided free medical care by general practitioners but not by hospitals or specialists (Stevens 1966:36). These services provided some care for the poorer half of the population, whereas the other half of the population had either to pay fees as private patients or depend upon voluntary sick clubs for medical care.

These various health services were seen to be inadequate, and proposals for full health and medical services were the subject of many reports in the years between World War I and World War II. It was the Second World War, however, that precipitated a major reform in health care services. All levels of English society at this time were united as never before in their agonizing struggle for survival. For the first time many physicians became aware of the need for reform. To deal with the war wounded, the Emergency Hospital Service utilized both voluntary and municipal hospitals for treatment and hospitalization of war casualties. In effect, Britain established in 1939 what was virtually a national hospital service to meet the needs of the war; moreover, it was because of this act that many of the leading physicians from prestigious teaching hospitals, involved in this war-time care, saw for the first time the poor conditions in many of the hospitals run by local authorities as well as in some of the voluntary hospitals (Abel-Smith 1972). Both the medical profession and the government agreed, in the early years of the war, on the need for reform of civilian health services. There was some disagreement about details regarding organization of such a service, but the principle of establishing a national health service was never an issue among Great Britain's political parties. In 1941 a committee was set up under Sir William Beveridge to survey the existing national schemes of social insurance and make recommendations as to the reconstruction of social services after the war. The committee's report, *Social Insurance and Allied Services: Report by Sir William Beveridge,* known as the "Beveridge Report," was published in 1942. The Beveridge Report recommended many changes that involved considerable extension of health and social services and formed the basis for much post-war social legislation.

In 1943 the government announced its acceptance of the proposal in the Beveridge report: that a comprehensive health service for all purposes and all people should be established under the supervision of the Health Department (Social Insurance and Allied Services: Report by Sir William Beveridge 1942–48). The 1945 election put a Labour government into power and Aneurin Bevan into the Ministry of Health, a combination that assured the acceptance of, first, a free health service for the entire population regardless of income and, second, the nationalization of the hospitals. The final plan was embodied in the National Health Service Act of 1946, and it began to operate on 5 July 1948.

The purpose of the National Health Service (NHS) is (1) to provide a system of medical services directed towards the achievement of positive health, the prevention of disease, and the relief of sickness, and (2) to render available to every individual all necessary services, both general and specialist, both domiciliary and institutional (Murray 1974:30). When introduced, the NHS was an immediate success in that almost everyone used the service and the great majority of doctors chose to participate in the system. Today only a small minority of specialists, about 2 percent of general practitioners and a negligible number of dentists, pharmacists, and opticians, take no part whatsoever in the NHS.

The National Health Service

Some of the important concepts of the structure of the health service are:

1. *Financing.* The National Health Service is financed from the following sources: 88 percent of the funds are derived from general taxation (Exchequer funds), 9 percent from NHS weekly contributions, 2.5 percent from co-payment by patients for certain services such as drugs, eyeglasses, and so on, and 0.5 percent from miscellaneous sources.

2. *Benefits.* The NHS pays for virtually the entire range of health and medical care, and care is free to the patient at the time of service without regard to age, income, need, or insurance qualification.

3. *Practitioner Service.* This service includes the family doctor service (general practitioner), the dental service, the ophthalmic service, and the pharmaceutical service. Patients register with a general practitioner and receive most primary services through him. Patients have a free choice of physician and are free to change doctors if they so desire. The practitioner is also free to accept or reject a particular patient. Throughout Britain, 97 percent of the population is registered with a family doctor. There are

some small charges made for dentures, eyeglasses, and patients usually pay a charge of 20 pence (35¢) for each prescription item. Certain groups of people such as children under 16, expectant mothers, men aged 65 and over, and women 60 years of age and over are exempt from these charges.

4. *Hospital Services.* All forms of hospital care and treatment are provided free of charge by the NHS. As a rule, patients are referred by their family doctors, who make arrangements with a specialist for their treatment and care in the hospital. In general, the family doctor does not have hospital privileges, but he may visit the patient in the hospital. All hospital services such as X-ray, laboratory, and rehabilitation services (physical therapy, speech therapy, and occupational therapy) are available free of charge to the patient.

5. *Community Health Services.* The care of patients in the community has been emphasized in Britain, and community services are well developed. The NHS provides a wide variety of community services, including maternity and child health services (family planning, midwifery, and baby care), home nursing, health visitors, vaccination and immunization, ambulance services, and health education for the public. During the past 26 years, there has been considerable progress in the development of health centers staffed by general practitioners, dentists, district nurses, and health visitors (registered nurses) to provide services for the prevention of illness as well as for general medical, dental, and pharmaceutical services. The traditional role of the health visitor centered on mothers and young children; however, increasingly she has been utilized in the care of old people in the community (Brocklehurst 1975).

6. *Payment for Services to Health Personnel.* Hospital doctors and personnel are salaried employees. Their salaries are set by the government and are standard throughout the country. Hospital consultants (specialists) may be part-time or

full-time; part-time staff are usually remunerated at a proportion of a full-time salary and are free to accept private patients. Senior hospital consultants earn salaries ranging from £7,500 to £10,700 a year (about $17,600 to $25,000 United States currency, as of December 1975). A general practitioner is paid a capitation fee for each patient on his patient list. A physician may maintain a list of up to 3,500 patients, but the size of the average practice is 2,400 patients. As of October 1966, a special payment has been made to general practitioners for every person aged 65 and over on their practice lists. Additional payments are made for practicing in doctor-shortage areas, for accepting responsibility for patient care out of normal hours, for night visits to patients in their homes, and for expenses associated with a rural practice. The British Medical Association estimated that as of April 1973 the average net income of the general practitioner was $14,300 annually and the average net income for top specialists was $19,000 (Committee on Ways and Means 1976).

Geriatric Care in Britain

The National Health Service Act of 1946 made it possible to promote geriatrics as a new specialty in medicine (Brocklehurst 1975). Geriatric medicine is concerned with the clinical, social, preventive, and remedial aspects of illness and the maintenance of health in the elderly (Anderson 1976). Although the NHS provided a structure for the organization and financing of geriatrics, progress in the care of the aged really began in the late 1930s, before the establishment of the NHS.

During the nineteenth century and extending into the early part of the twentieth century, many aged, because they were poor, received health care through the Poor Law hospital system. Many of the workhouses had adjoining hospitals or infirmaries, and in 1906 45 percent of the workhouse inmates were 60 years of age and over (Townsend 1962). Under the Local Government Act, 1929, the Poor Law infirmaries gradually began to be appropriated by health departments of the local governments, which were already responsible for the mental hospitals, infectious disease hospitals, and tuberculosis sanatoria (Stevens 1966:59). It was in these beds that the emerging specialty of geriatric medicine began to develop in the late 1930s.

The person who is generally regarded by British geriatricians as the pioneer in geriatric medicine is the late Dr. Marjorie Warren. In 1935 Dr. Warren was given the task of reorganizing the treatment of several hundreds of aged, chronic sick at the West Middlesex Hospital in London. The hospital had taken over the adjacent Poor Law infirmary that housed hundreds of old people along with children and healthy and infirm patients. Dr. Warren, described by those who knew her as an exceptional woman totally ahead of her time, realized the infirmary contained large numbers of patients who were inadequately diagnosed and improperly treated. Conditions in such infirmaries, which have since been termed "human warehouses," were dreary and depressing, and the patients' morale was very low. Most had lost hope of ever recovering. Dr. Warren began by classifying patients under her care: the ambulant were sent to welfare hotels, the ill were grouped together and given thorough medical treatment, the infirm were encouraged to be more active, and the frail were studied to determine the cause of their weakness. Dr. Warren attended not only to their physical needs, but their mental and social needs as well. Wards were redecorated in light, bright colors, and new furnishings made the rooms look clean and cheerful. Subsequently, patients became happier and began to have hope for recovery. People who had been categorized as chronically ill began to improve and return to reasonable health and activity, fewer and fewer beds were needed, and Dr. Warren began to develop a special geriatric unit with about one-third of the beds she originally had taken over (Howell 1963). Her unit became a model for geriatric care, and visitors came from throughout the country to observe and learn so that they might develop similar facilities. Many physicians were influenced by the enthusiasm and common-sense approach of Dr. Warren. Today geriatrics is a recognized specialty in Britain.

Many medical schools include the teaching of geriatric medicine in their medical school curriculum; the University of Glasgow has been teaching geriatric medicine in the school of medicine for the past 25 years. British geriatricians believe there is a sufficient body of knowledge within the specialty of geriatrics to make it a worthwhile subject and that emphasis should be given to the subject in the teaching of medical students at all stages in their training. A Chair in Geriatric Medicine has been created in universities in Belfast, Birmingham, Edinburgh, Glasgow,

London, Manchester, and Southampton; and this has greatly encouraged the development of teaching in geriatric medicine (Personal Interview Professor Sir Ferguson Anderson 1977).

Community Services

The philosophy of geriatric care in Britain is that old people should be kept in their own homes and as independent as possible for as long as it is feasible.[1] This has been possible because of the extensive development of community and social services since the inception of the NHS. The domiciliary services include: home helpers (domestic assistants who aid the aged with household tasks such as shopping, cooking, and cleaning), meals-on-wheels, home nursing service, volunteer friendly visitors, podiatry services in the home, home physiotherapy, and occupational therapy (Anderson 1976).

Community services also include various levels of housing accommodations for the elderly who are unable to remain in their own homes. These facilities are provided by the local government or voluntary agencies; proprietary or commercial interests are not involved.

Sheltered housing has proved a most satisfactory solution for old people who wish to maintain some degree of independence but also need some supervision and attendance. In this type of living arrangement, the elderly reside in small, apartment-type units that allow them to have their own furniture and belongings and to organize their lives as they wish. A matron (often a registered nurse) lives in the complex, makes daily rounds to visit all of the residents, and is always available through a call system should the aged resident need help.

Residential homes are available for those who are more dependent, that is, for those who are unable to prepare their own meals and carry out certain aspects of their personal care. To qualify for residential care, prospective residents should be able to walk, feed, and dress themselves without assistance; and they should be continent of urine and feces. Residential homes are primarily staffed with domestic help only; if nursing care is needed the person should be transferred to an appropriate medical facility. However, while visiting a residential home or a sheltered housing project, the matron would periodically single out an elderly resident who

---

1. Although institutional care is the primary focus of this study, a brief discussion of community services is necessary for a broad understanding of geriatric care in Britain.

"should be transferred" because she could no longer care for herself, but, in fact had not been transferred because the matron knew the patient was very attached to the home. She felt the move would be harmful to the resident. The matrons I met in these homes were, without exception, dedicated and one might even say devoted to the elderly residents. The aged were obviously very fond of them, and the matrons cared very much for their elderly residents.

The Geriatric Day Hospital

The geriatric day hospital is another service for the aged in Britain that helps keep old people in the community; it prevents unnecessary hospital admissions, and in some cases it allows the patient to be discharged from the hospital at an earlier date. The first purpose-built[2] geriatric hospital opened in Oxford in 1958, and by 1970 there were 120 established day hospitals in Great Britain and Northern Ireland (Brocklehurst 1970). The day hospital is open five days a week, and patients are brought into the hospital by an ambulance provided by the National Health Service.

Day hospitals must be differentiated from day centers. Day centers are usually run by the local authority, by voluntary groups, or by both, and they primarily provide social and recreational activities and a hot cooked meal at midday. The geriatric day hospital has a therapeutic focus, providing rehabilitation care (physical therapy, occupational therapy, and speech therapy), maintenance treatment, and medical and nursing care. Patients who have been seen in the home by a geriatrician may come into the day hospital for further examination or for X-rays and laboratory tests. Geriatricians have found that frequently an elderly patient, who may be reluctant to leave his home and be admitted to the hospital as an in-patient, will agree to come to the day hospital for out-patient diagnosis, treatment, and rehabilitation. It is also more economical to care for the elderly on an out-patient basis.

Although the day hospital is primarily therapeutic, social aspects of care are also taken into consideration. Patients arrive at the facility between 8 A.M. and 10 A.M. and are immediately served tea and biscuits. There is a beauty salon in the hospital; some of the women may have a shampoo and hairset while waiting to see the geriatrician. At lunchtime

---

2. "Purpose built" is a British expression that is roughly equivalent to our "built for the sole purpose of . . . ."

they are served a hot meal, and at 2 P.M. tea and biscuits are served before they return home. Patients with physical disabilities may be brought to the day hospital for purely social reasons. A physical disability may isolate an elderly person in the community, and perhaps because of this disability, he cannot utilize the day center. The opportunity to join other elderly people in a pleasant social environment is beneficial to a person who may have few, if any, other social contacts.

The geriatric day hospital is a very successful, progressive concept in the care of the aged patient. Many elderly people have multiple chronic illnesses that require maintenance treatment and rehabilitation. If this care is not provided, the aged person's condition will frequently deteriorate to a point where institutionalization in an acute or continuing care unit becomes necessary. The geriatric day hospital is another means of keeping the aged person independent and in his home for as long as possible.

The Geriatric Service

Completing the spectrum of care for older people in Britain, the geriatric service, using Dr. Warren's pioneering work as a model, has been organized throughout the country in the past 25–30 years. The geriatric service comprises three types of wards: assessment, rehabilitation, and continuing care. When an old person becomes ill, either in his own home or in special housing, the general practitioner is called. General practitioners make home visits when necessary and determine if the patient needs to be seen by a geriatrician. If so, in most circumstances the elderly person is assessed at home by the geriatrician. A junior member of the medical house staff occasionally makes the assessment visit, but this initial contact is considered so important that most geriatricians do not delegate it to others. Most geriatricians agree that the patient is best assessed at home; thus, an evaluation of the family and home conditions, as well as a clinical medical assessment, can be made at the same time. This home visit gives the consulting geriatrician a complete picture of the aged person in a natural setting, and it is helpful later on in making discharge plans. It is also of great value in developing rapport between the old person and the new doctor, the hospital consultant. Another reason for making a home assessment visit is that the demand for geriatric beds usually exceeds the available supply; thus, the consultant responsible for the patients can establish priorities for admission to the geriatric unit. If it is necessary to have a further diagnostic examination/treatment following the home visit, the person is admitted to the geriatric unit.

In her early work, Dr. Warren strongly advocated that geriatric units be an integral part of the general hospital, that they not be divorced from the mainstream of medicine. In providing care for the geriatric patient, therefore, geriatricians not only have access to all hospital services, such as X-ray, laboratory, and physiotherapy, they also have immediate access to consultants in other specialties. If necessary, patients can easily be transferred to another unit for treatment and care. For example, in one instance the geriatrician had been asked to see an elderly woman who was referred as a "social problem" because she was no longer able to walk. She was admitted to the geriatric unit and upon examination was found to have a tumor on her spine. The patient was immediately transferred to a surgical unit, surgery was performed, and following rehabilitation, the patient could walk again and returned to her home.

Assessment Ward

The assessment ward (also called the acute geriatric unit) receives patients from their own homes or from community residential facilities. Of those admitted to the assessment ward, 46 percent return to their own home, 36 percent are discharged to rehabilitation or continuing care units, and 18 percent die (Brocklehurst 1975). The average length of stay on the assessment ward is two to three weeks, and the emphasis is on diagnosis and treatment. Social workers assist in the investigation of the patient's social problems and help in the assessment planning of the patient's future. It is impressive to observe the number of people who function as a team in the geriatric unit. The team consists of the geriatrician, supporting medical staff, nurses, physiotherapists, occupational therapists, diversional therapists, chiropodists, speech therapists, social workers, community liaison nurses, and secretarial staff. There is a strong spirit of cooperation and interdependence, and geriatricians acknowledge that a "team effort" is not only desirable but necessary for them to plan and carry out the best possible treatment and long-term goals for the elderly patient.

Rehabilitation Ward

The rehabilitation ward receives most of its patients from the acute geriatric ward, but some patients are also admitted from medical, surgical, and orthopedic units. Treatment in the rehabilitation ward, again, is very much a team effort; the emphasis throughout is on physical, social, and mental rehabilitation. The average length of stay on the rehabilitation ward is two to three months. Approximately 57 percent return to their own home or an old people's home, 27 percent are transferred to a continuing care unit, and 16 percent die (Brocklehurst 1975).

Continuing Care Ward

If after a period of time on the rehabilitation ward, it becomes apparent that the patient is not going to achieve the necessary physical or mental independence to return home, he is admitted to a continuing care unit. These units were previously called "long-term units," and some health care professionals continue to use this term; however, recently an attempt has been made to change the terminology to "continuing care." There is concern that the elderly and their family will feel abandoned by the professional health care team, and it is felt the term "continuing care" will convey to the patient and the family that everything possible is being done to keep the aged patient as healthy, normal, and independent as possible. The majority of the patients who are admitted to the continuing care ward remain there until their death; this ward becomes their final home.

The preceding pages have presented an overview of the ideal structure of the geriatric service in Britain. While one geriatric department may differ from another in minor ways, this common pattern of progressive care is found in most areas. Although British geriatric medicine has made great progress since the 1940s and British Geriatric Care is considered among the finest in the world, development of the service has been uneven throughout the country. The geriatric service is not without its problems. For example, there is a shortage of British-trained geriatricians as well as a shortage of appropriate beds and facilities for the aged. The provision of comprehensive geriatric care in the community still remains problematic in some areas.

Despite the tremendous growth in the number of geriatricians, from four or five in 1948 to more than three hundred at the present, recruitment of physicians to the specialty of geriatrics remains a problem. Geriatrics is still seen as a low-status specialty, and this stigma contributes to a shortage of British-trained geriatricians. Many consultant appointments in geriatric medicine are filled with graduates of foreign medical schools (Brocklehurst 1975:34), yet in England and Wales in 1975, 10 percent of the geriatric consultant posts were unfilled (Report of the Working Party of the Royal College of Physicians of London 1979).

A shortage of facilities at all levels of care (residential homes, sheltered housing, continuing care hospitals, and beds in acute hospitals and in geriatric units) contributes to a host of problems. Many patients are discharged to their homes because there is no available space in residential homes, yet they must leave the hospital to make room for the more acutely ill elderly waiting to come in (Brocklehurst 1978). Complaints are frequently made that elderly patients are blocking beds in acute medical and surgical wards. Rubin and Davies (1975) found the reason elderly patients were remaining longer than necessary in acute wards was the length of waiting lists for alternative residential housing.

The lack of appropriate accommodations also contributes, in part, to misplacement of the elderly. Carstairs and Morrison (1971), for instance, studied all of the homes for the aged in Scotland and found that, of the total group of 10,906 residents, 61.4 percent would be more appropriately placed in sheltered housing, 15.3 percent were considered more properly placed in residential homes, 11 percent would be more suitably placed in a home for the mentally infirm, and 11.9 percent belonged in a hospital.

Adequate provision of medical care following hospitalization has also been identified as a problem. The failure of the family practitioner to provide follow-up care is well documented. Brocklehurst and Shergold (1969) found that 47 percent of the patients discharged from two geriatric units had no contact with their general practitioner during the first month after leaving the hospital. This immediate post-hospital period is considered critical in the patient's care.

There are other problems in the care of the elderly in the community. Williamson et al. (1964) have drawn attention to a considerable amount of undiagnosed physical illness in elderly persons in the community. Similarly, there is a high incidence of unrecognized mental illness among the elderly, both in the hospital and in the community (Bergman et al. 1965; Bergman and Eastham 1974). Underlying many of these problems is a shortage of financial resources. Many of the buildings occupied by the elderly are old and unsuitable; the majority were built in the nineteenth century (Brocklehurst 1975). Financial resources are also necessary to provide additional community services for those elderly who, with supportive care, could remain in their homes. Yet despite these deficiencies, the progressive and innovative concept of British geriatric care provides an interesting model for comparison with long-term geriatric care in the United States.

Historical Development of Health Care Services in the United States

The development of medical care in the United States, although more recent than that in Britain, is also more varied and difficult to characterize. The roots of American medicine can be traced to England and the Continent. American medicine relied heavily on the scientific leadership of England and Scotland until about 1820; then France, and finally, after the Civil War, German universities provided American doctors with training that enabled them to establish research centers at medical schools in the United States (Stevens 1971:55).

Among the early practitioners who came to the colonies were a small number of physicians holding university degrees, but for the most part the colonial physicians had no formal training; more commonly, they were ships' surgeons and others who became doctors through apprentice training (Shryock 1960:7). These beginning practitioners took on apprentices of their own and thus apprenticeship became the chief mode of education for physicians. In a colonial world dominated by fevers, infections, malnutrition, and very high mortality rates, New England ministers and southern planters acted as both lawyers and physicians, and schoolmasters and other educated men were forced, out of necessity, to dispense medical advice (Stevens 1966:12). All of these practitioners were termed "doctors," but in fact they resembled the surgeon-apothecaries of rural Britain.

The absence of a metropolitan or university focus in the colonies, the prevalence of "domestic" medicine, and the training of physicians through apprenticeship discouraged the stratification that occurred between the university-trained physicians and the nonuniversity-trained surgeons and apothecaries in Britain. The categories of physicians, surgeons, and apothecaries that existed in England until the nineteenth century never developed in the United States. The apprenticeship system encouraged the development of an all-around bedside practitioner who practiced medicine, surgery, midwifery, and also dispensed his own drugs. Indeed, for many physicians the dispensing of drugs became necessary for financial survival (Stevens 1966:14).

In summing up medicine in early colonial America, one can say that disease conditions were more serious than in Europe, that inadequate as European medical science was, it reached the colonies only to a limited degree. During this time medical care was largely ignored by both the church and state, and voluntary services reflected an unplanned adaptation of British tradition to the American situation (Shryock 1966:7).

In the United States in the seventeenth, eighteenth, and nineteenth centuries, medicine as a profession developed slowly. In Paris between 1750 and 1850, hospitals began to be used for research, thus forming a center for the development of medical science; in Britain, hospital expansion also began before 1850. In the United States, however, there was no widespread development of hospitals before the 1880s, nor was there a strong professional medical organization to initiate reform (Stevens 1966:10).

Rapid urbanization and immigration brought about the further development of hospitals in the major cities in the late nineteenth century; at the same time, these same two factors created slums that contributed to massive outbreaks of infectious disease. Thousands of impoverished immigrants poured into the seaboard cities of New York and Boston, where the inadequate provision of housing, water supplies, sewage disposal, and drainage produced an urban environment similar to the slums in London and other English cities. During the nineteenth century, there were repeated epidemics of cholera and yellow fever, and at the same time other infectious diseases such as smallpox, typhus, typhoid, dysentery, diphtheria and scarlet fever were causing high mortality rates.

Chadwick's 1842 Report profoundly affected Americans who were concerned with public health conditions; clearly, Lemuel Shattuck's *Report of the Massachusetts Sanitary Commission* (1850) drew heavily upon the work of Chadwick. But whereas Chadwick's report led to the passage of the Public Health Act of 1848 in England, in the United States the Shattuck Report had practically no immediate effect. One of its major recommendations—that a state board of health be established to deal with the urban health conditions—was not implemented until 19 years later. Shattuck also recommended the establishment of a state health department and local boards of health in each Massachusetts town. He stressed the need for smallpox vaccination and advocated well-child care and school health and mental health programs. The farsightedness of this report is illustrated by Shattuck's proposals on smoke control, alcoholism, town planning, and the teaching of preventive medicine in medical schools. Although a farsighted man, Shattuck was limited by contemporary political and social trends; he died in 1859 after unsuccessful attempts to have the Report enacted into law (Rosen 1958:240–43).

The lack of government involvement in matters of public health in the

United States contrasts sharply with the government's involvement in Great Britain. Whereas in Britain there was national responsibility for public health in the latter part of the nineteenth century, in the United States the federal government took little action in public health matters. Community health was considered the responsibility of state and local governments. Throughout the nineteenth century, the only involvement of the U.S. government in public health functions was that carried out by the Marine Hospital Service (founded in 1798) to care for sick and disabled seamen (Brand 1965:237). The American political philosophy, with its emphasis on states' rights, delayed any national action for public health until it became clear that state and local governments were unable to handle many health and welfare problems. In 1878 a severe outbreak of yellow fever in the Mississippi Valley, causing great loss of life, brought forth a public demand for action. In the following year Congress created a temporary National Board of Health responsible to the President. This agency was so unpopular that four years later, in 1883, Congress, imbued with the concept of states' rights, failed to pass a reenactment bill. Incredible as it seems, not until 1953, 70 years after the demise of the National Board of Health, was an independent, national health agency established in the United States. The Marine Hospital Service (renamed by Congress in 1902 the Public Health and Marine Hospital Service, and 10 years later again renamed the United States Public Health Service) was based in the Treasury Department until 11 April 1953, when it was transferred to the newly created Department of Health, Education, and Welfare (Rosen 1958:469).

The reluctance of the federal government to become involved in public health matters can also be seen in the lack of government action in personal health care in the United States. In the early part of the twentieth century, a number of organizations studied the development of social security plans that covered the working population for accident insurance, old-age pensions, sickness insurance, and health benefits. With the encouragement of President Theodore Roosevelt, the first federal workmen's compensation act was passed in 1908 for civil employees; between 1910 and 1915 workmen's compensation laws were passed in thirty states. Health insurance was considered the next logical step; under the leadership of the American Association for Labor Legislation and with the support of the American Medical Association (AMA), a standard health insurance bill was introduced in fifteen states in 1917. But no health insurance act became law. In the meantime, opposition to compulsory health insurance had rallied within the medical profession, commercial insurance companies, and other groups. The governmental role in compulsory health insurance was seen as undesirable paternalism, and compulsory health insurance was attacked as being socialistic, tyrannical, "un-American," and "German" (Stevens 1966:138).

Following World War I, at a time when compulsory health insurance was commonplace in Europe, the AMA increasingly opposed government health insurance. In the Sheppard-Towner Act of 1921, the AMA faced yet another governmental action in health care; this act authorized federal money to states for the improvement of the health of mothers and children. The AMA opposed this act in 1921 and its renewal in 1926. The Association said the act threatened states' rights and endangered the fabric of the American home; under increasing opposition from the AMA, attempts to renew the act in 1931 and 1932 were unsuccessful. It was not until the Social Security Act of 1935 that federal-state programs for maternal-child health were reborn.

During the Great Depression many people were unable to pay their medical bills; hospitals were in serious financial trouble and many closed. The Hill-Burton Act of 1946, which provided funds for hospital construction and modernization of hospitals, was the most important piece of health legislation in the post-war period (Stevens 1966:269). Still, any proposal of a truly national health insurance had little chance of being endorsed by the AMA. Rather, the AMA endorsed hospital insurance (Blue Cross) and committed itself to private health insurance.

By 1967, 76.6 percent of the civilian population had some form of private insurance coverage. Voluntary health insurance (as opposed to compulsory or government health insurance) combined with private, fee-for-service practice, became the dominant characteristic of financing personal health in the United States. Voluntary insurance grew rapidly after World War II as health insurance became a part of fringe benefits, and fringe benefits acquired a new importance in the collective bargaining of labor unions. Millions of workers in the steel and auto industries received health insurance coverage in this way; moreover, the medical association used this enormous growth of voluntary health insurance to argue against a national health insurance plan. Numerous bills for national health insurance died in Congress in the 1940s. In 1945 President Truman took a strong position in advocating national health insurance; the legislation he proposed would have produced a compulsory, comprehensive national health insurance system. The AMA labelled the bill as "regimentation" and "totalitarianism," and Senator Robert Taft called it "the most socialistic measure that this Congress has ever had before it": the bill did not pass (Stevens 1966:272).

It was not until 1965, with the enactment of Medicare (for the aged) and Medicaid (for the poor), that the federal government assumed a major role in the financing of health care in the United States. Earlier, federal health activities had been limited to traditional public health functions; the support of medical research; and the provision of medical care for the military, for veterans, and for merchant seamen who were cared for in Public Health Service hospitals. With the financing of Medicare and Medicaid, the federal expenditure for health care has increased dramatically. Before these two programs went into effect in 1965, annual federal expenditures in health were about $4.4 billion; in 1970 the total was $18 billion, and current figures show that "indirect" health services, in which Medicare and Medicaid are the dominant elements, cost $35.7 billion in a total health budget of $49.6 billion in 1977 (Walsh 1978).

Home Health Services

In the United States the primary emphasis in health care services has been in acute short-term care and long-term institutional care. In contrast to Great Britain, the U.S. has not supported and developed home health services. In recent years public funds for nursing home care (institutional care) have increased markedly. In 1960 total revenues for the industry were $500 million, by 1970 they had increased 460 percent to $2.8 billion, and by 1974 revenues from all sources had reached an estimated $7.5 billion (Special Committee on Aging, United States Senate 1974). In fiscal year 1977, $12.5 billion was spent for nursing home care (Kane and Kane 1978). While expenditures for institutional care have increased sharply, expenditures for home health services under Medicare and Medicaid have remained very low. Utilization of home health services in the Medicare system has remained at less than 1 percent of insurance expenditures. In 1973 home health services accounted for about .7 percent ($64 million) of all Medicare expenditures. Home health services under Medicaid in 1973 amounted to $24 million or about .3 percent of all expenditures for Medicaid recipients (Reif 1977).

As mentioned above, home health services are not well developed in the United States. There is no comprehensive range of services readily available and accessible, and the current range of services do not meet the most pressing needs of the elderly population. Services are oftentimes fragmented; indeed, the public, as well as many health care professionals, is uninformed about the types of services available and where to go to obtain necessary assistance.

One of the greatest problems in the provision of home health care is the lack of funding for those services most often needed. To qualify for in-home health services, the person must need professional nursing or some other type of skilled professional care such as physical therapy. Services are provided primarily to those patients who are likely to improve or be rehabilitated; care of the "custodial" patient is specifically disallowed under Medicare. The total number of visits for all types of services is even limited to one hundred visits under Medicare, Part A, as a post-hospital service and one hundred visits per year under Medicare, Part B, with no requirement of prior hospitalization for those who can afford co-insurance (Special Committee on Aging, United States Senate 1972). Since the number of visits allowed includes visits by all personnel (nurses, physical therapists, social workers, and others), this plan in effect provides only for short-term care following an acute illness. Many of the same limitations that apply to Medicare home health benefits also apply to Medicaid. Medicaid emphasizes limiting home health care to those individuals who are acutely ill. In short, the elderly patient must be sick enough to require skilled professional services, but not sick enough to require too many visits or too much care. Medicare and Medicaid do not provide funds for those who most need services, the chronically ill with some degree of functional impairment.

Coverage for home health services by private insurance companies is uneven, limited, and frequently more restrictive than the coverage provided by Medicare. Charitable organizations make a significant contribution to the funding of home health care, but these contributions are not sufficient to provide assistance to the extent needed (Reif 1977).

There are considerable restrictions and deficiencies in home health services in the United States; consequently, thousands of elderly people are needlessly institutionalized because they need some relatively inexpensive assistance with homemaking services or other home health care that would enable them to remain in their home (Special Committee on Aging, United States Senate 1972).

The Growth and Development of the Nursing Home Industry

The lack of home health services and the emphasis on institutional care in the United States has brought about a tremendous increase in the number of institutionalized elderly in recent years. The number of nursing homes increased from 9,582 in 1960 to 23,000 in 1976, a 140 percent increase, and the number of nursing home beds increased 302 percent from 331,000 to 1,327,358 (Moss and Halamandaris 1977:7). Out of this increase a veritable industry has grown: the nursing home. Total expenditures for nursing home care have risen from $1.75 billion in 1967 to $12.5 billion in 1977 (Hickey 1980, Kane and Kane 1978).

Since there are many types of institutional facilities for the aged that provide a variety of services, a brief explanation and a definition of terms is in order at this point. Among the various types of long-term facilities are nursing homes, convalescent hospitals, convalescent homes, board and care homes, rest homes, and county homes. All long-term-care facilities provide one or more of the following services: (1) nursing care such as administration of medication, catheterizations, dressing changes, and other procedures under the direction of a physician; (2) personal care such as bathing, grooming, dressing, and assistance in walking and eating; (3) residential care, that is, room and board, laundry, and other personal amenities. The emphasis in the long-term-care facility is not on restoration, rehabilitation, and return to the community; some 80 percent of the aged who enter these institutions die there rather than in their own homes (Butler 1975). Instead, these long-term-care institutions exist primarily as permanent placement facilities, as do the continuing care wards or hospitals in Britain.

Of the various types of long-term-care institutions in the United States, the nursing home is the predominant institution, the one most frequently referred to in discussions of institutional care, both in professional and lay literature. A nursing home, as defined by the American College of Nursing Home Administrators, is an institution providing a protective and supervised environment, licensed to care for those persons who because of physical or mental conditions require a combination of health care services, personal services, and living accommodations that can best be made available through institutional facilities other than acute-care units of hospitals (Nursing Home Fact Book 1971). These services may include skilled nursing care, medical care, assistance with medications and therapeutic diets, regular observation of the patient's physical and mental condition, personal assistance with bathing, dressing, grooming, walking and household activities, and a program of social and recreational activities.

Although the historical antecedents of the nursing home are somewhat difficult to trace, it appears that almshouses—the public poor houses of colonial America—were the historical progenitors of nursing homes. In both Britain and the United States, the care of the aged has been historically intertwined with the care of the poor and the destitute. In the early part of the eighteenth century, workhouses were established in England for the employment and maintenance of the poor, who were refused relief if they would not enter the workhouse (de Schweinitz 1943:63). By 1732 over fifty such workhouses had been built in England, and most of the larger colonial cities followed the mother country: Philadelphia in 1732, New York in 1734, and Charleston in 1735. Even after political separation, in 1788 New York state used the English Poor Law of 1722 as a model when it required each town to establish an almshouse (Freymann 1974:24). Although the original intent of the Poor Law legislation was to confine the able-bodied poor, it was usually cheaper and more efficient to confine all welfare cases, the sick, orphans, the insane, and the aged in the same workhouses. The proportion of aged in the workhouses in Britain and in the almshouses in the United States increased over the years because of a reduction of the children and able-bodied adults and because the number of old people in the population was increasing rapidly. In 1906, 45 percent of all the workhouse inmates in England were persons 60 years of age and over; of the 140,000 elderly persons in Poor Law institutions, only one or two thousand were in separate establishments for the aged (Townsend 1962).

In the United States the almshouses served as the place of last resort for parentless children, for the mentally retarded and the insane, for the aged who were infirm, and for strangers in the community who had no family and who had suddenly fallen ill (Rothman 1971). Special institutions were developed in time to care for the various categories of dependents who had been housed in the almshouses. In New York, for example, Bellevue took over the care of the acutely ill poor in 1848, the blind were removed from the workhouses in 1831, the mentally retarded in 1851, children in 1875, and the insane in 1890. By World War I, the almshouse population was down to the aged, the infirm, and the chronically ill (Freymann 1974:20).

As immigrants poured into the U.S. in the nineteenth century and as the cities grew large and crowded, the almshouse appeared to be the perfect solution to the problems of unemployment and poverty. As the cities grew larger the almshouses also grew, both in numbers and in size. Conditions within deteriorated rapidly. In the state of New York, a committee investigated every city and county almshouse in 1857, and reported that nearly every one was badly constructed, poorly heated and ventilated, and that dependents, regardless of age, sex, or condition were crowded together in small, filthy rooms. Overcrowding was endemic. In one almshouse near Bellevue Hospital, officials desperately made lofts and basements into dormitories to make room for fifteen hundred residents. The investigators told the legislature that the great mass of poor houses were the most disgraceful memorials of the public charity, that domestic animals were usually more humanely provided for than the paupers in some of these institutions (Rothman 1971).

It was because of strong public reaction to conditions in the public poor houses that Congress, with the enactment of the Social Security Act of 1935, prohibited the payment of federal old-age assistance to any individual housed in public institutions. The effect of this legislation was the displacement of thousands of elderly people from public facilities to proprietary boarding homes. The proprietary home provided the only means by which welfare administrators could evade the law, thus privately owned, profit-making nursing homes were in a seller's market and grew rapidly: the nursing home industry was born (Freymann 1974:29–32).

The 1935 Social Security Act, one of the earliest major social welfare programs, provided the impetus for the beginning development of long-term-care facilities. For the first time in American history, people over the age of 65 had a guaranteed monthly income that enabled them to pay, at least in part, for some type of proprietary living accommodations, and this increased the demand for long-term-care facilities. By the mid-1950s, the number of homes for the aged had grown substantially, but the greatest growth came in 1965 with the enactment of Medicare and Medicaid. Nursing home regulations were established, and these regulations led to the disappearance of some of the smaller homes and the development of larger homes as big business, including several national hotel and motel chains, entered the field (Freymann 1974:31). In 1973, 74 percent of the homes and 68 percent of the beds were proprietary, 22 percent of the beds were in nonprofit institutions, and 10 percent were in government institutions (Kane and Kane 1978). Within a few years, the nursing home industry had grown to a multi-billion dollar industry. Today it is the primary institution for the care of the chronically ill aged.

In the eighteenth, nineteenth, and the early twentieth centuries, many of the aged in both Britain and the United States received long-term care in the Poor Law hospital system or in public almshouses. Although both countries recognized that the care in these public poor houses was inadequate, and in many cases even disgraceful and inhumane, the approach to the care of the elderly in each country is due at least in part to the financing, organization, and philosophy of health care.

Beginning in the late nineteenth century, there was in Britain a national responsibility for public health; the 1911 National Health Insurance Act provided some personal medical care for the poor. During the early years of World War II, the medical profession and the government agreed on the need for reform in health services, and a plan for comprehensive health care for all people was embodied in the National Health Service Act of 1946; it began to operate on 5 July 1948. The express purpose of the NHS was to provide a comprehensive system of medical services directed toward the promotion of health, the prevention of disease, and the relief of illness through a wide array of institutional and community services. The NHS provided a structure for the organization and financing of geriatric medicine and made it possible to promote geriatrics as a specialty.

In the United States, by comparison, there has been a lack of government involvement both in matters of public health and in personal health care. Although there has been support for national health insurance by some political groups, it has been met by strong opposition to compulsory health insurance from the American Medical Association. Not until 1965, with the enactment of Medicare and Medicaid, did the federal government assume a major role in the financing of health care. Thus, whereas the National Health Service Act of 1946 made the British government responsible to establish a comprehensive health service, in the United States there is no plan to coordinate health care. That there is no central responsibility for care (as pointed out in Chapter 6) contributes to the low quality of care in many American nursing homes.

The difference in philosophy of health care in the two countries is also significant. In Britain, both philosophically and practically speaking, medicine in general and geriatric medicine in particular, have been concerned with the clinical, social, preventive, and rehabilitative aspects of health care, which concern has been to the advantage of the elderly. Today the geriatric service, in cooperation with social services, provides a comprehensive range of institutional, community, and domiciliary services to the elderly. In the United States the primary emphasis in health care services has been on acute, short-term, hospital-based care. The lack of interest in chronic, rehabilitative community care and services has been to the disadvantage of the elderly. There is no comprehensive range of services readily available, and the present range of services does not meet the most urgent needs of the elderly. For many of the chronically disabled elderly, the nursing home is often the only available option for care.

8

Exchange Theory – Theoretical Interpretation

The preceding three chapters have analyzed those factors that may in part be responsible for the lower quality of care at Pacific Manor. However, this analysis does not fully reveal why the United States, a country that prides itself on excellence in acute care, will tolerate such low standards (and sometimes even inhumane care) in the care of the institutionalized aged. I should like to propose that exchange theory might offer some insight into the problem and perhaps explain on a theoretical level the difference in the care of the elderly in the two institutions.[1]

Exchange refers to the transaction of labor, resources, and services within a society and plays a vital part in the social life of all societies. "Exchange is not limited to economic markets: social exchange is ubiquitous" (Blau 1968:453). Malinowski (1922), in his description of the kula, and Mauss (1925), in his analysis of gift exchange, were the first anthropologists to observe this phenomenon, and they have greatly influenced the development of exchange theory. In addition to Malinowski's analysis of the Trobriand kula ring, anthropologists have examined other social institutions, such as bridewealth in African societies and the pot-

1. Some readers may suggest that the data could be analyzed using other theoretical frameworks such as social organization, social class, or network theory. I have chosen to limit the theoretical discussion to exchange theory because I believe that the principles of exchange theory more than any other theoretical framework help to explain the interpersonal relationships and other phenomena observed in this research.

latch of the North American Indians. These institutions illustrate reciprocity, which is the prevailing and characteristic mode of exchange, and demonstrate the essentially social nature of a reciprocal exchange of valued goods. Sociologists and social psychologists such as Homans (1961), Emerson (1962, 1972), Blau (1964), and Ekeh (1974) have also made major contributions to exchange theory.

Dowd (1975), drawing upon the work of Emerson and Blau, has put forth a view of aging as a process of social exchange; he sees the problem of aging as one of decreasing control over power resources. As power resources decline, the aged, unable to engage in balanced exchange relations, are forced to exchange compliance for their continued sustenance.

Major Propositions of Exchange Theory

Some of the major propositions of exchange theory as set forth by Emerson (1962, 1972) and Blau (1964) include:

1.   People enter into social relationships because they expect them to be rewarding.

2.   A person who derives benefits from another is under obligation to reciprocate by supplying some benefit in return.

3.   When an individual fails to reciprocate, there is no incentive to continue to befriend him and he is likely to be accused of ingratitude.

4.   When the person does reciprocate, both parties benefit from the association, a social bond develops between them, and the interaction between the two will probably be continued.

5.   In every interaction, costs are inevitably incurred. Cost is defined as the resource one gives to the other party. If one perceives the cost to be equal to the reward, the exchange relationship is in balance.

6.   If one participant values the rewards more than the other, an imbalance results and the latter person has power over the former—a unilateral dependence develops.

Power is the ability of persons or groups recurrently to impose their will upon others, despite resistance, through deterrence either in the form of withholding regularly supplied rewards or in the form of punishment (Blau 1964:117). By supplying regularly needed services to others who cannot reciprocate, a person establishes power over them and they are forced to comply with his wishes. In power-dependence relations, individuals who need services have the following options: (1) they can supply a service in return, (2) they may obtain the service elsewhere, (3) they can use coercion to obtain the service, (4) they may choose to do without the service. If they are uanble to choose any of these alternatives, they must comply with the wishes of the one in power since he can make the continuing supply of the needed service contingent upon compliance.

Application of Exchange Theory to the Institutionalized Aged

The propositions of exchange theory cited above are especially relevant to the care of the institutionalized aged.[2] Owing to their physical disability, mental impairment, and (for some) lack of friends and relatives, many are dependent upon staff for multiple services. But since they have few resources with which to reciprocate, they are forced to comply with the wishes of the staff. Mrs. Lundgren, for example, is dependent on the staff for bathing. She objects to being placed in the shower room with male patients. "I don't know how the men feel," she averred, "but I find it disgusting! But what can I do?" None of the options mentioned above is open to her. She is too disabled to perform a return service for staff, she cannot obtain the service elsewhere, she has no power of coercion, and she cannot do without the service. Her only alternative is to comply with their wishes because she realizes that if she complains they can withhold the service.

The institutionalized aged are clearly dependent on staff for services. Staff can render these services promptly, willingly, and respectfully; or they can use the situation to exercise power over the aged. I found, for instance, that at Pacific Manor there are more examples of staff exercising power over patients than at Scottsdale. I submit that this occurs because the American patients have fewer resources and are more dependent: they are unable to engage in balanced social relationships.

2. This theoretical analysis will necessitate repeating previously discussed descriptive data.

Dependency of the Aged at Pacific Manor

The atmosphere of an institution and the quality of its care can either maximize one's level of functioning, thereby promoting independence; or conversely, it can mimimize one's level of functioning and make one dependent upon others. At Scottsdale, for example, a portable telephone at wheelchair level can be placed in patients' rooms (every room has a telephone jack); patients can independently and privately talk with friends and relatives. But at Pacific Manor the only telephone is in the hallway at a level unreachable for those confined to wheelchairs; they must depend upon staff to dial the phone and they cannot talk privately.

The quality of medical and nursing care also contributes to patients' dependence or independence. At Scottsdale medical problems are given prompt attention, yet at Pacific Manor they may go untreated for weeks. On one occasion the director of nursing service at Pacific Manor asked me to visit Mrs. Edwards, who was depressed and had not left her room for days. While visiting with me, she confided that she had been troubled with diarrhea and urinary frequency for weeks but that she could get no attention from the nurses or doctor. This patient had only one kidney, she had repeated urinary tract infections, and she was frightened about her condition. A very proud woman, she was not going into the lounge for coffee and activities because she was afraid she would not get back to the bathroom in time and would wet herself. "I've told the nurses," she said, "but they don't do anything about it. If I had the courage, I would go to the telephone and call my doctor myself." "What do you mean?" I asked. "I'm afraid to walk that far because I might not get back to the bathroom in time," she explained. Even though she stayed in her room, she was sometimes incontinent and then dependent upon the staff to change the bed linens. Also, she could no longer independently get her morning coffee. As I walked into the lounge to get some for her, the activity director said, "I would rather that you not take coffee to Mrs. Edwards. She is just too lazy to come out of her room." I explained the situation and added, "I would like to take coffee to her; she's such a lovely woman." "I think she's obnoxious," the director replied. "She doesn't like the programs I have arranged for the patients and has been complaining that they are not as good as they used to be." This incident provides a clear example of staff exercising power over a patient who had become dependent upon them for a service.

At Pacific Manor some patients were restrained in chairs (forced dependency), were incontinent because they were not taken to the bathroom, and were made to wait several hours before their clothes were changed (compliance). At Scottsdale, by comparison, I never observed patients restrained in chairs. The nurses made rounds every 2 to 3 hours, offered bedpans to some, and walked those who were able to the bathroom.

Lack of Resources

A lack of resources also creates dependence and contributes to an imbalance in social exchange relations. Resources are essentially anything perceived by the exchange partner as rewarding; it may be a skill, money, or food—anything that someone has and the other values or wants. Resources enable one to reciprocate in an exchange relationship; they serve as an inducement for staff to furnish service and protect patients from dependency and compliance (Blau 1964:119).

The patients at Scottsdale have more resources than do patients at Pacific Manor. As mentioned in Chapter 3, they make items in diversional therapy that are valued by the staff and others. Mrs. Frazer, for example, knits beautiful sweaters and scarves (she can hardly keep up with the demand) that she sells at a reasonable price to staff and friends. Others make lovely trays, padded coat hangers, and children's toys, which they sell or give to staff and relatives. These items provide patients with resources they can give in exchange for services. This in turn enables them to engage in balanced exchange relationships. It is unlikely that a nurse will treat Mrs. Frazer unkindly when she is knitting a sweater for that very nurse. These exchanges also contribute toward the establishment of social bonds.

In addition to making products for exchange, the Scottish patients have money and access to a shop where they can purchase articles to give to others. Most have only a basic government pension as income, which must go toward the payment of their care. Nevertheless, patients are permitted by law to keep £3.05 per week (approximately $6.00) for personal use. By American standards this may seem like a small amount, but because they are provided with virtually everything ("they want for nothing," remarked one of the nurses), it gives them considerable purchasing power. On several occasions I observed patients giving treats to a "special nurse," and I, too, was the recipient of such gifts. Patients valued my lengthy visits. On some days, in fact, I began to feel guilty as I collected chocolate bars, biscuits, coat hangers, and homemade marmalade. The marmalade provides an interesting example of a successful exchange system. The minister of one of the Scottish women made delicious orange marmalade. Each time he came she ordered several jars, which he delivered on his next visit and which she in turn gave to staff who were especially kind to her. "I am good to people who are good to me," she smiled.

By contrast, patients at Pacific Manor have few resources. Since they are not able to engage in any productive activity, they have no products that they can exchange for services. Additionally, many are without money; 50 percent of the Pacific Manor patients, who were formerly private patients, are now on Medicaid. They have become impoverished through their long-term illness. Although Medicaid stipulates they be permitted to keep $25.00 per month for personal use, the likelihood of theft keeps them from having money in their rooms. Some keep a small amount in the business office, but there is no shop in the facility where they can purchase food and sundry items.

It was intriguing to observe that, despite the restrictive environment at Pacific Manor, some of the elderly managed, through their ingenuity, to develop balanced social relations with certain staff members. Mrs. O'Sullivan has no family and her closest friend, an 84-year-old woman, lives fifty miles away. Her needs are small; she likes potato chips and mints for snacks and a little wine now and then. Fortunately, she has a skill that she can exchange for service. Mrs. O'Sullivan alters and mends clothes for one of the nurse aides, who in turn shops for her. "Of course, I wouldn't charge her for it," she said. "When I can do her a bit of a favor I do, and when she goes to the store and I need something, she shops for me."

Mrs. Levine is one of the more fortunate patients. She has an attentive daughter and numerous friends who visit frequently and provide her with money and food, which she carefully hides and uses to purchase favors. She does not like to go to the hair dresser, for example, who charges $6.00, and she does not like to wait in line. So she has arranged for one of the aides to wash her hair, and she in turn pays $1.00 for this service. Mrs. Levine always has resources available and carefully reciprocates. When I took her some of her favorite cheese, she immediately offered candy in return.

Mrs. Crawford, a 93-year-old woman with no relatives but many friends, has been one of the most resourceful and successful in establishing balanced exchange relations. I was in her room one day when a nurse aide came and asked for some food. "I always come in for something to eat when I go on my coffee break," she explained. "Mrs. Crawford always has nice things in her room." Mrs. Crawford said she had received four big boxes of candy and many homemade Christmas cookies. "There was plenty for everyone," she beamed, "and I share it with all the girls." Her favorite nurse aide was Mrs. Lee. "She is so good to me," Mrs. Crawford went on. "When anything is bothering me, I always tell Mrs. Lee; she is like a sister to me." When Mrs. Lee's son was in the hospital, Mrs. Crawford sent him a box of candy. A strong social bond has developed between these women, and Mrs. Lee (a powerful woman because of her long tenure at the nursing home) will not permit anyone to speak unkindly of Mrs. Crawford. On one occasion staff members were saying how mean Mrs. Crawford had been because she had attacked a male orderly and scratched his arm. Mrs. Lee immediately went to her defense: "He tried to 'manhandle' her," she corrected them, "so she scratched him."

Mrs. Crawford is an outgoing person who likes people and needs companionship. The food she keeps in her room provides an incentive for staff to come in for a brief visit. Because of her generosity, furthermore, she has made many friends among the staff and appears to be somewhat exempt from the theft problem. Although other articles have been stolen from her, the food, which she keeps in large tin boxes right at the head of her bed ("most things get taken at nighttime," she said) usually is not disturbed.

Negative Exchange

Although social exchange by and large concerns a reciprocal giving and receiving of goods and services, some theorists have included negative exchange as an element of social exchange. Homans (1961:57–61) speaks of exchanging punishment, Blau (1964:227–30) and Kiefer (1968:225–44) refer to offenses that call for retaliation, and Sahlins (1965:148–49) and Price (1978:339–50) discuss "negative reciprocity." Although our conceptualization of negative exchange lags behind that of positive exchange (Befu 1977:259), I believe it may explain some of the negative staff-patient interaction seen at Pacific Manor. For example, there are many elderly persons at Pacific Manor with few resources who require long-term care. In our culture they are seen by the productive members of society as useless, dependent, and nonproductive; they are a burden and a nuisance. Clark (1972:267) discusses how one who becomes a burden is seen as having nothing of value to exchange; he is in a nonreciprocal role. If an individual is arbitrarily defined as having nothing of value to exchange, moreover, he is expecting something for nothing, and in our culture, with its strong emphasis on self-reliance, negative sanctions are usually brought against such persons (Clark 1972:270). The infantilization, depersonalization, dehumanization, and victimization described earlier illustrate the negative sanctions brought to bear against those who are in nonreciprocal roles.

Negative Reciprocity

Sahlins (1965:148–49) defines negative reciprocity as "an attempt to get something for nothing with impunity." Haggling, gambling, chicanery, and theft are some of the various means used by some to profit by another's expense. This concept of negative exchange may explain the theft of patients' belongings that occurs at Pacific Manor. The poorly paid staff, who have no social bonds with the patients, victimize them for personal gain because punishment is highly unlikely. The elderly cannot retaliate; their families may complain but their complaints are not acted on, and the administration does not see theft as an important problem. Thus it is advantageous for staff to steal from patients; they can do so without recrimination.

Retaliation

Some of the punitive behavior discussed earlier in the infantilization, depersonalization, dehumanization, victimization process suggests that the staff may retaliate in their treatment of the elderly. In both institutions staff commented on the dependency of patients. "They want us to do everything for them; they come in here and forget they have hands and feet," said one nurse. A staff member at Pacific Manor clarified, "They have been catered to for so many years; they become dependent and think we are here to provide services for them." Although the importance of encouraging the elderly to be as independent as possible (most prefer this) is widely recognized, it must also be understood that, because of unavoidable circumstances, many are dependent on others for some of their care. I believe that staff do resent the work involved in the care of dependent patients and further resent that they are poorly paid to perform difficult work; at Pacific Manor, many approach their work sullenly as a result.

Resentment on the part of the staff may be caused by their poor working conditions. The personnel at Pacific Manor are exploited by the institution. They are among the lowest paid health care workers in the U.S., and their salaries compare unfavorably with those of similar workers in acute-care institutions. Blau (1964:229) suggests that "exploitation and oppression are punishing experiences which arouse anger, disapproval, and antagonism." If a person is severely deprived, he feels a strong desire to retaliate by harming those who have harmed him. In this situation, however, employees cannot retaliate against the proprietor, who controls their salary; predictably, they take out their resentment on the patients. For example, an incontinent patient may be considered difficult and uncooperative. The incontinence creates more work for the staff, and they punish the patient for this "extra" work by not changing the linens promptly.

Because many of the elderly at Pacific Manor do not have resources, it would be beneficial for them if social bonds could be established in other ways. Functions wherein staff, patients, and their friends and family interact on a social level is one suggestion. Staff would begin to see patients as individuals and treat them more kindly; it is more difficult to be unkind to those whom one knows personally. But it must be kept in mind that the depersonalization of patients by the staff may be a protective mechanism. It is emotionally taxing to care for people who will not get well; the mortality rate is high at Pacific Manor. If staff become personally involved with patients, it may be painful to see them die.

The behavior observed on a staff-patient level must also be examined on the societal level; for, broadly speaking, exchange theory is also applicable within the socio-cultural context of each country. Every society, after all, determines what is a fair exchange, and there is common agreement on the terms of exchange. For example, for more than 30 years (since the beginning of the NHS) the British people have agreed that they will pay taxes in exchange for health care services. This is considered by virtually all of the people to be a fair and equitable exchange. Hence, the elderly are not receiving any special consideration. Like everyone else in the society, they are entitled to health care; one government-financed system exists for all.

In the United States, by contrast, the prevailing attitude toward medical care is that one is individually responsible and must pay privately for health care through an insurance program or from personal funds. Those who cannot pay in exchange for health care services are thought to be unworthy of receiving high-quality care. They may procure care through government-financed programs, but these programs are considered welfarism by many Americans, and those who must participate in such programs are considered second-class citizens. Many people in our society (which stresses individual responsibility for health care) feel such individuals receive something for nothing; hence, they should rate lower-quality care and they must accept what is offered without complaint. Unfortunately, many of the elderly, who have become impoverished through long-term illness, fall into this classification.

This attitude of what is fair exchange on a socio-cultural level exerts a subsequent impact on an institutional and individual level. For example, as reported in Chapter 6, physicians at Pacific Manor, products of our society, often provide only minimal care to the institutionalized elderly in exchange for Medicare and Medicaid payments. Taking his cue from the attitude of society in general and physicians in particular, the owner of the institution knows that he need provide only minimal care to the elderly in exchange for payment. He will not be held accountable by professionals or society. Subsequently, the poorly paid nonprofessional staff observe this behavior on the part of those who should be responsible for care. They are fully aware that the elderly are seen by others as undeserving of a high standard of care and conclude that they need provide only minimal service in exchange for their substandard pay. Consequently, the elderly become the victims of the system, whereas the nursing home industry, owing to a lack of professional responsibility and an absence of effective public pressure realizes tremendous profits.

9

Institutional Barriers to Quality Care: Concluding Thoughts

The preceding chapters have discussed some of the major differences in the care of the aged in an institution in Scotland and one in the United States. From this discussion it is apparent that the elderly at Scottsdale receive higher-quality care; consequently, they are more satisfied with institutional life than their counterparts in the American institution. In this chapter I shall be concerned with the institutional barriers to quality care for the aged. From my observations it appears that the lower quality of care at Pacific Manor stems largely from three problems: (1) there is a lack of leadership and responsibility by professionals (doctors and registered nurses) for the care of the aged; (2) accountability for care at Pacific Manor is not to health professionals; it is to the proprietor of the institution, who hopes to make a profit and who is in turn accountable to the State Department of Health to avoid being closed for violations of regulations; and (3) the organization and financing of health care contributes to the pauperization and stigmatization of the aged.

Lack of Leadership and Professional Responsibility

Although some professionals question the advisability of providing long-term care for the aged under a medical rather than a social model, the fact remains that most elderly people in long-term-care institutions have multiple medical problems and functional disabilities that require continuing medical and nursing care. It seems desirable therefore that nurses and physicians, the primary providers of that care, should be in leadership positions and work cooperatively with other health care workers to meet the health and social needs of the institutionalized aged.

Medical Care

There is ample data in the preceding chapters to indicate that medical care at Pacific Manor is at a minimal level and that the aged feel neglected because of the infrequent and perfunctory visits of their physicians. Most doctors make only the state-required monthly visit (if that), write a brief note on the chart, and take little or no interest or responsibility for the rehabilitation and continuing care of the aged. As a nurse I have worked many years in acute-care hospitals, and it is difficult for me to imagine that physicians in acute-care facilities would tolerate the inhumane treatment and the incompetent care I observed daily at Pacific Manor.

In the United States physicians have clearly abdicated their responsibility in the care of the institutionalized aged; multiple reasons have been given for their disinterest and lack of responsibility. Butler (1975:179) believes physicians share our culture's negative attitude toward old age: they fear, deny, and avoid the issues of aging, dying, and death. Moreover, the doctor's need to cure (which makes the care of the acutely ill person more attractive than the care of the chronically ill), inadequate reimbursement, and the failure of medical schools to teach geriatrics are other explanations that have been offered for physicians' failure to care for the institutionalized aged (Butler 1975:178; Moss and Halamandaris 1977:172–78). Although all of these factors contribute to inadequate medical care, I believe the major institutional barrier contributing to the lack of responsibility and leadership by physicians in the care of the institutionalized aged is the failure of medical schools to include geriatrics in their curricula.

Failure of Medical Schools to Teach Geriatrics

It is incredible that in the United States, with its rapidly increasing number of aged and with the increasing specialization in medicine (82 percent of the active physicians are specialists), there is no specialty in geriatric medicine. Yet not only do the majority of medical schools presently fail to include geriatrics in their curriculum, they also indicate that there is little interest in establishing geriatrics as a specialty (Butler 1975:181; Moss and Halamandaris 1977:173). Indeed, this attitude is difficult to understand when the older age groups, who have cumulative, multiple pathology, obviously have the greatest need for medical care. If there is a need for pediatrics and obstetrics as a specialty, logically, there is a need for specialization in geriatrics. The tragedy of this situation is that many of the elderly are either misdiagnosed or deprived of medical care and forced to live with medical problems that are preventable and treatable. Because geriatrics is not taught in medical schools, some physicians are unable to cope competently with the problems of advanced old age. "If they have not been taught how to diagnose and treat mental impairment while a student, they are terrified and run away from it when they see it in practice," noted one of Scotland's leading geriatricians. The absence of geriatrics in the medical school curriculum also conveys to medical students, at a very impressionable time in their lives, the idea that the care of the aged is not an important part of medicine. This in turn contributes to the negative image of old age in our society and to the abandonment of the aged in institutions.

The lack of support for geriatrics as a specialty in most medical schools in the United States contrasts sharply with Scottish Academic Medicine. Although it is still a controversial subject, a growing body of Scottish physicians strongly believe there is a sufficient body of knowledge to warrant including geriatrics as an academic subject in medical schools (Anderson 1976; also personal interviews with staff consultants Anderson, Wilson, and Kennedy in 1977). These specialists also believe it is important for medical students to visit the elderly in the community, on acute geriatrics wards, and in long-term facilities.

Although geriatrics is not a preferred specialty in Scotland, and some physicians there also abhor old age and death, a group of concerned, competent, and energetic physicians has succeeded in establishing geriatrics as a specialty and has provided outstanding leadership in geriatric care. Geriatricians have worked diligently to raise the status of the field by establishing geriatric chairs in major universities (e.g., the Universities of Glasgow and Edinburgh), by setting high standards in the training of future geriatricians, and by establishing geriatric units in major teaching hospitals. The successful recruitment of young doctors into geriatrics is due partially to the fact that there is much competition for consultancy posts. As mentioned earlier, a physician in Britain elects to be either a consultant (i.e., a specialist) or a general practitioner; by far the majority must go into general practice. Consultants are attached to major teaching hospitals and the number of posts in each specialty is limited, especially in popular areas such as surgery or obstetrics. As a result, a physician may have to wait several years to obtain a post, in the meantime working at a much lower salary as a staff physician. This disproportionate "supply and demand" has "encouraged" physicians to enter geriatrics. Although their motives may not be altogether altruistic, once in geriatrics, most of these new specialists are enthusiastic about and happy with their choice. I visited with geriatricians in three Scottish cities, and all of them spoke of the advantages geriatrics had to offer: they had become consultants at a very young age, their salaries were equal to those of other consultants, and they found the field challenging and rewarding. "Because of the multiple pathology found in old age, it is challenging to practice geriatric medicine," said a junior geriatrician at Scottsdale. "It is one specialty where you can treat the 'whole' person."

Although Scottish physicians may achieve professional status and financial gain by choosing geriatrics as a career, there are no such incentives in the United States. In fact, the reverse is true. In the United States the financing and organization of health care have concentrated money and power in hospitals, where the focus of care is the acutely ill patient, whereas such matters as chronic conditions and community service are underfinanced and undervalued. There is more money and status in acute care, and consequently the aged, many of whom suffer from long-term, chronic conditions, are neglected. Physicians in the United States enjoy high social status as well as very high incomes (Chapman 1978:851). Time is money to them; if there are no financial incentives for them to care for the institutionalized aged, many will not do so. In fact, the medical director at Pacific Manor confided that financially it was not worth his time to visit his patients there.

Well-qualified professional nurses also will not work in a nursing home when they can earn a higher salary at an acute-care hospital (see Chapter 6). Like the physicians, they earn more money and enjoy a higher status in acute-care nursing. Hence, in the absence of professional responsibility, the proprietor makes administrative decisions that determine the level of care, and the provision of care is largely in the hands of poorly paid nonprofessional staff.

This absence of professional involvement contrasts unfavorably with the Scottish situation. At Scottsdale, without question, the chief geriatrician exercises authority; he has high standards for care, and the nursing staff cooperate with him to meet those standards. For example, if a patient who had been neglected at home came in with a pressure sore, a concerted effort was made to heal it. The geriatrician believed that if the patient were kept off his back, the bedsore would heal. "I want that patient off his back 24 hours a day," he ordered, "and I don't mean 23 hours and 59 seconds, but 24 hours a day!" Such concern and professional responsibility were never voiced at Pacific Manor during my research there.

Teaching geriatrics in medical schools would help awaken doctors to the special needs of the aged; however, if nursing homes continue to remain outside the mainstream of medicine, conditions are not likely to improve significantly. Nursing homes presently fall under the jurisdiction of the state only: there is no formal health care structure to enforce professional standards. In Scotland, government inspections are carried out by the Scottish Home and Health Department. The chief geriatrician is additionally responsible for the care of the elderly in all geriatric institutions within a defined geographic region, and his reputation as a physician depends upon the quality of care in these institutions. By contrast, in the United States the care of the aged has been left primarily in the hands of the state and private entrepreneurs concerned with making a profit.

Accountability for Care to the Owner

Important institutional barriers to quality care for the aged in the United States are the American philosophies of individual responsibility and private enterprise rather than a blanket governmental responsibility for the provision of health care. Although Medicare and Medicaid are government-financed health programs, in keeping with our philosophy of free enterprise they are financed through private insurance companies. In the United States 74 percent of the nursing homes are privately owned (Kane and Kane 1978); obviously, nursing home care has become a commercial enterprise, and profit making, even at the expense of the disabled aged, is considered a legitimate goal. Profit making is the primary goal at Pacific Manor, where accountability to the proprietor is a major concern for the administrative staff.

Unfortunately for the aged, the emphasis on financial gain is often directly opposed to high-quality care. "We cannot have a selective menu," explained the dietician; "that would greatly increase the cost of food service." "We cannot take patients on outings on a regular basis," the activity director went on; "the cost of insurance to cover the possibility of accidents is very high, and if I did it without insurance and the owner heard about it, he would have my head." Also, as mentioned in Chapter 3, there is no budget to provide social and occupational activities; most patients are idle throughout the day while others are engaged in meaningless activities, such as bingo, which can be offered at virtually no cost. The profit-making motive also interferes with hiring practices. "I cannot compete for well-qualified staff because of the low salaries we pay," said the director of nursing service. When new state legislation required that nurse aides take classes and pass an examination to obtain certification for employment in the nursing home, the director of nursing service was concerned primarily about what it would cost the proprietor to give them time off to attend the classes. She expressed no concern about how much they would learn or if this knowledge would improve patient care. It was a requirement that had to be met in the cheapest way possible.

Clearly, when the goal of an institution is to make money, decisions will be made in favor of profit making rather than on the basis of what is best for the patient. This is especially likely to occur when many of those being served are incapable of protesting, have no alternatives or recourse, and when there is little concern on the part of the staff. I asked patients in each institution "If you had a complaint about your care, to whom would you speak?" At Pacific Manor one woman said, "I don't know; I would just pray about it." Another added, "I don't know who to go to. I really don't know. I am not the complaining kind. My niece said it isn't good policy to say anything; you just make enemies. She said I should just put up with it." And a third woman agreed, "I never complain about anything, I just get along." In response to the same question, the Scottish patients said they would complain either to the sister, the matron, or their doctor, and the problem would be resolved.

Since there is a lack of professional responsibility, the proprietor of the nursing home has much decision-making power, and this has negative effects for the aged. For example, the monetary resources of the aged are given to a third party, the proprietor, who should pay staff a reasonable salary and hold them accountable to provide quality care. Yet the proprietor, knowing that professionals have abdicated their responsibility, defaults; he underpays staff and fails to hold them answerable. The elderly are short-changed and victimized in the process, not only by staff but by the proprietor as well.

Accountability to the State

When feeling especially frustrated on one occasion, the director of nursing service reflected, "I spend all of my time thinking about how to save money so we can make a profit and how to prepare for the visit from the state." As mentioned in Chapter 7, with the advent of Medicare and Medicaid, the number of nursing home beds increased dramatically. Many of the small proprietary homes were substandard; consequently, the State Department of Health has spent a great deal of time, money, and effort in the development of minimum standards. Although there are regulations covering every conceivable aspect of care from staffing to the minutest detail of the physical plant, unfortunately these regulations often contribute minimally to the quality of care. In fact, because bureaucracy focuses on technical aspects more than on humanitarian goals, the state inspections may actually contribute to a decline in the quality of care. The time and energy of the staff is diverted away from patient care toward meeting the state requirements; the state, in effect, becomes yet another "master" to be served. For instance, the director of nursing service at Pacific Manor is so occupied with filling out official forms, meeting state-set standards, and preparing for Health Department personnel visits that she has little time for patient care, does not supervise nursing care, and does not even know most of the patients by name.

Several factors contribute toward making the nursing home inspection something of a farce: the staff are informed in advance of the state inspection visit, inspections are conducted in a pro forma manner, and it is difficult for the state to enforce citations. "The state is coming today," the director of nursing service announced to the staff one morning, "so don't throw your linens on the floor, and make sure the nurse in charge is around when trays are being passed, because they are checking on that." I observed a state inspector interview a patient about her care. The patient spoke not a word in response to the inspector's questions, yet the inspector filled out a lengthy form.

A remarkable observation I made during the field work is that a nursing home can check out satisfactorily on all 600 items included in the inspection, but the care it offers may still be of very low quality. To illustrate, the state requires that the nursing home have the service of a dentist available for patients, and Pacific Manor has contracted a dentist to provide dental services. A dentist is defined by the state as "A person licensed as a dentist by the Board of Dental Examiners." I inquired about this service because one of the patients had no teeth and was being served pureed food. "We have a dentist on the staff," confirmed the assistant administrator, "but he's a butcher; at least I wouldn't let him touch my teeth." The state also requires that "Facilities shall employ a registered nurse or a licensed vocational nurse eight hours per day on the day shift, seven days per week." Pacific Manor meets this requirement on paper; however, this does not assure quality nursing care. As a case in point, one of the registered nurses was thought by other staff members to be an alcoholic; she spent a great deal of time at the desk and in the staff bathroom, and very little time with patients. Although formally qualified, she clearly was an unsatisfactory staff member.

Again, state regulations include several pages of directives carefully outlining policies and procedures for an activity program. They define "activity program," the qualifications of personnel to organize and direct the activities, the scope of the activities to be included, the number of hours a week there are to be activities, and so forth. In response to these directives, a calendar of events is posted each month at Pacific Manor, and if an inspector were to look at this schedule it would, indeed, appear that all of the patients are actively involved. In reality, however, there is little meaningful activity for patients. At Scottsdale, ironically, there is no activity director, yet patients there are active and express satisfaction with the programs; at Pacific Manor there is an activity director, yet patients are idle, bored, and dissatisfied with the programs offered. The state requirements, although well intended, obviously contribute little toward the quality of care.

Organization and Financing of Health Care: Pauperization and Stigmatization of the Aged

A major institutional barrier to the provision of quality care for the aged is posed by Medicare and Medicaid. Despite efforts to avoid classifying recipients of Medicaid as charity patients by allowing them to use private rather than public facilities and by channeling payment for services through private insurance companies, Medicaid has become synonymous with welfarism. Those who receive it bear the stigma that has traditionally been attached to welfarism. The crux is that to qualify for these programs many nursing home patients must exhaust their savings and be reduced to poverty. In fact, in *The Aging Enterprise* (1979) Estes notes that over 47 percent of nursing home costs are paid by Medicaid for patients who were not initially poor (U.S. Congress 1977).

It is devastating and humiliating for the elderly to be forced to go on welfare in their old age. Clark (1967:177–80) found that the elderly placed a high value on physical and financial independence; they were proud and did not want to become a burden to others in their old age. As mentioned earlier, 50 percent of the patients at Pacific Manor are on Medicaid. All of them had previously been privately financed patients, but they have used all of their savings to pay their bills and are now on welfare. Some complain bitterly that the institution has taken all of their money. "I had money when I came here, but now it is all gone," said Mr. Franklin. "They have taken all of my money," said Mrs. O'Sullivan. "I paid for my care when I first came, but now I am on Medicaid." Others feel that their status has been diminished in the process. "I feel just like a pauper," said Mrs. Levine. "When I realized they were bringing me here, I thought to myself, it is like going to the poor house." Mrs. LaSalle also said, "I feel just like a pauper." "What do you mean?" I inquired. "Well, I have nothing," she said. "I had to sell everything. I had a lovely home and lovely furniture and now it is all gone." Mrs. LaSalle had been admitted following a cerebrovascular accident; I thought perhaps with physical therapy she might be able to leave the nursing home. "What will you do in the future now that your house is gone?" I asked. "There is no future," she said.

Not only do patients feel like paupers, but staff members also seem to look upon them as such; this may in fact be responsible for the inhumane treatment described in Chapter 4. In our society poverty is still associated with personal failure, and those who are poor are considered lazy and undeserving of care. Moreover, illness is considered by some to be a punishment for sin. All this places the aged, who are old, sick, and poor, in a very unfavorable position. It is not surprising that they receive inferior care. We cannot classify them as second-class citizens and expect them to be given high-quality care.

Because the present system of financing long-term care for the aged forces them into virtual poverty, I believe our nursing homes have become modern-day poor houses. To qualify for care, the elderly lose their possessions and many of their rights, and in turn they are provided with minimal care. Townsend's description of life in the old workhouse bears a remarkable similarity to conditions at Pacific Manor: "Few of the residents wear their own clothing or retain more than a few belongings. The diet is plain and there is almost no choice of menu . . . there is little attempt to cater for individual needs and tastes. Religious and social activities are organized, but few residents participate. Most lead an extremely self-contained existence, rarely conversing with anyone" (Townsend 1962:97–108). He also notes that patients were not allowed to keep money and that matrons and wardens had considerable power and were unnecessarily authoritarian. This unattractive vignette precisely describes the environment at Pacific Manor. History, it almost seems, has repeated itself.

Although American medicine has made tremendous progress in biomedical research in the past 30 years, we have made little progress in our approach to the delivery of long-term health care services for the aged, nor does our present system compare favorably with that of Britain. This is not to say that all of the elderly in Britain are receiving excellent care or that the geriatric service is operating successfully in all parts of the country. Still, Britain has recognized the need and taken the necessary steps to develop the institutional structures that guarantee at least a minimum of care for the elderly; and in some cases, such as at Scottsdale, an excellent program of care for the institutionalized aged has evolved.

After considerable thought, I am convinced that, without similar facilitative structures and without concerned professionals to take the responsibility for implementing an organized plan of care, the chronically disabled elderly in the United States will not receive quality care.

It is somewhat disconcerting to conduct research and realize that the solutions to the problems identified are multiple, complex, and infeasible without major institutional changes. The pauperization of the aged by Medicaid, for instance, can be averted only by legislative action that would restructure the financing of health care. Proprietary nursing homes in many cases are not oriented toward quality care for the aged; however, even if they were taken out of the hands of private ownership and placed under the auspices of the government, our doing so would not guarantee quality care for the aged. The failure of medical schools to teach geriatrics could be resolved if medical schools would include geriatrics in their curriculum. But this specialty may be difficult to implement because of the strong academic emphasis on acute care and the lack of interest and financial support for chronic, long-term care. I believe the medical profession has a responsibility to contribute toward the improvement of the care of the institutionalized aged. It is irresponsible to prolong life and subsequently take no responsibility for the quality of that life.

Nurses can contribute a great deal toward alleviating the problem, and therefore I strongly recommend: (1) that geriatric nursing be included in the curricula at both the undergraduate and graduate level of nursing education; (2) that schools of nursing prepare geriatric nurse practitioners for leadership roles in long-term-care institutions; (3) that salaries of nursing staff (professional and nonprofessional) be made equal to, if not higher than, those of nurses in acute-care settings. However, here again, the problem of profit making comes to the fore. Proprietary institutions assert they cannot pay higher salaries because the per-patient Medicaid payment is not high enough to allow them to make a profit; this is a dilemma that will be difficult to resolve. But, if nurses, through the mechanism of their professional nursing organization, established a policy that no nurse would work at a substandard salary, nursing homes would have to comply. Nurses, however, cannot function independent of the physician; there must be collaboration and cooperation between responsible physicians and nurses for the good of the elderly patient.

The purpose of my research was to investigate criteria for quality care and to discover what conditions within and without long-term-care institutions will encourage the maintenance of high standards of care. Although difficult to duplicate in the United States without a national health service, the Scottish model of geriatric care provides an excellent example of quality long-term care. By comparing Pacific Manor to Scottsdale, I have found that we cannot impoverish the aged, deprive them of virtually all their resources, place them in an institution that lacks professional leadership and accountability, and at the same time expect poorly paid professional and nonprofessional staff to give them quality care. The only organized attempt (the establishment of federal and state regulations) to deal with the problem of inadequate care has had some positive effects, but it does not really address the issue of quality care. It is foolish and nonproductive to establish detailed state regulations to upgrade nursing homes and, subsequently, staff those very institutions with poorly qualified people. The most important ingredients in the provision of care are competent staff and accountability for care. Accountability for care must be present at all levels; it cannot be the responsibility of the state alone. Auxiliary staff ought to be accountable to health care professionals who are academically and clinically prepared to provide care for the elderly. The accountability for care must begin and be present within each individual nursing home.

Quality care for the institutionalized aged is neither difficult to define nor costly to provide. In comparison with acute care, which often involves expensive diagnostic medical and surgical procedures, long-term care is not costly. Primarily, long-term-care institutions should provide professionally competent and emotionally supportive staff, good food, meaningful activities, and some of the amenities of life. The aged need just what everyone else needs when ill: attention to their medical problems and physical needs and, especially, emotional support, because many are suffering from multiple physical and social losses. They need care, kindness, compassion, and understanding; and they need to be treated with dignity and respect. Meeting the needs of most of the chronically ill aged does not take a great deal of expensive and sophisticated equipment or diagnostic treatments and tests. To provide quality care, we must surround the elderly with an environment as normal and "homelike" as possible (permitting them to have some control over their lives) and we must demonstrate by our care that we value them as human beings.

At Pacific Manor the lack of medical attention, the absence of qualified nursing staff, the poor quality of food and activities, and especially the infantilizing, depersonalizing, dehumanizing, and victimizing treatment convey to the aged that they have no value; the effect this has on them is devastating and debilitating. The withdrawal, depression, loss of hope, and desire to die expressed by patients at Pacific Manor had no analogue at Scottsdale. The unpleasant environment at Pacific Manor was overwhelming even for the few who had considerable resources and who had worked out a fairly comfortable life in the institution. Mrs. Levine, for one, had weekly visitors and a devoted daughter who brought her special food and took her for outings several times a year. When she was not feeling well one day, I asked the nature of her illness; she replied, "Well, it's not too serious, I guess, I am afraid it is nothing that will kill me." She went on to say how very difficult it was to live in the nursing home. "I don't know why I don't die; I don't know why! I had such a good chance to die when they took me to the hospital; I was so sick. There's just no sense to living like this; this is not living. I don't know why I keep on; it is just terrible here, and I had such a good chance to die. I never talk to my children like this," she added. "There is no need to make their lives miserable; they are doing the best they can." It is disturbing to see patients so depressed with their living arrangements that death is all they can hope for; it is more painful for them to live than to die.

For some of the aged in our society growing old is painful. There is the physical pain of arthritis, the emotional and psychological pain of losing loved ones, and the pain and infirmity that accompanies the loss of sight and hearing and the ability to walk. But for some of our institutionalized aged, the greatest pain to be endured is that of an empty existence in an oppressive environment—surrounded by strangers and deprived of friends, possessions, and dignity. This pain causes even the strong to cry out: "I don't know why I don't die; this is not living."

It is too late to help the one million elderly who are currently institutionalized in the U.S., but will a similar despair also be our destiny if we become disabled in our old age?

References

Abel-Smith, Brian
   1972. Politics of Health in Great Britain. *In* Politics of Health, Douglass Cater and Philip R. Lee, eds. Pp. 197–214. New York: Medcom Press.

Aldrich, C. K., and Ethel Mendkoff
   1963. Relocation of the Aged and Disabled: A Mortality Study. Journal of the American Geriatrics Society 11:185–94.

Anderson, N., et al.
   1974. Policy Issues Regarding Nursing Homes: Findings from Minnesota Survey. Minneapolis.

Anderson, W. Ferguson
   1976. Practical Management of the Elderly. 3rd ed. Philadelphia: Lippincott.

   1977. Opening Address. *In* Age and Ageing 6, Supplement.

Befu, Harumi
   1977. Social Exchange. Ann. Rev. Anthropol. 6:255–81.

Bennett, Ruth G.
   1963. The Meaning of Institutional Life. The Gerontologist 3:117–25.

Bergmann, K., E. M. Foster, and D. W. Kay
1965. "The Need for an Integrated Geriatric Service in Psychiatric Disorders in the Aged." Geigy, Manchester.

Bergmann, K., and E. J. Eastham
1974. Psychogeriatric Ascertainment and Assessment for Treatment in an Acute Medical Ward Setting. Age and Ageing 3:174–88.

Beveridge, Sir William
1942. Social Insurance and Allied Services. American ed. New York: The Macmillan Company.

Blau, Peter M.
1974. Exchange and Power in Social Life. New York: Wiley.

1968. Social Exchange. *In* International Encyclopedia of the Social Sciences. Vol. 7, Pp. 452–57. New York: Macmillan/Free Press.

Blumer, Herbert
1969. Symbolic Interactionism: Perspectives and Methods. New York: Prentice-Hall.

Bourestom, N., and S. Tars
1974. Alterations in Life Patterns Following Nursing Home Relocation. The Gerontologist 14:506–10.

Brand, Jeanne L.
1965. Doctors and the State: The British Medical Profession and Government Action in Public Health, 1870–1912. Baltimore: The Johns Hopkins Press.

British Information Services
1974. Health Services in Britain, London: Central Office of Information.

Brocklehurst, John C.
1970. The Geriatric Day Hospital, London: King Edward's Hospital Fund for London.

1975. Great Britain. *In* Geriatric Care in Advanced Societies, J. C. Brocklehurst, ed. Pp. 5–41. Lancaster: MTP.

1978. Geriatric Services and the Day Hospital. *In* Textbook of Geriatric Medicine and Gerontology, J. C. Brocklehurst, ed. Pp. 747–62. New York: Churchill Livingstone.

Brocklehurst, J. C., and M. Shergold
1969. Old People Leaving Hospital. Geront. Clin. 11:115–26.

Butler, Robert N.
1975. Why Survive? Being Old in America. San Francisco: Harper and Row.

Butler, Robert N., and Myra I. Lewis
1977. Aging and Mental Health: Positive Psychosocial Approaches. St. Louis: The C.V. Mosby Company.

Camargo, O., and G. H. Preston
1945. What Happens to Patients Who are Hospitalized for the First Time When Over Sixty-five Years of Age? American Journal of Psychiatry 102:168–73.

Campbell, M. E.
1971. Study of the Attitudes of Nursing Personnel Toward the Geriatric Patient. Nursing Research 20:147–51.

Care of the Elderly in Britain
1977. Prepared for British Information Service by the Office of Information, London, R5858/77.

Carstairs, V., and M. Morrison
1971. The Elderly in Residential Care: Report of a Survey of Homes and Their Residents. No. 19, Scottish Health Service Studies. Edinburgh: Scottish Home and Health Department.

Chapman, C. B.
1978. Doctors and Their Autonomy: Past Events and Future Prospects. Science 200:851–56.

Cicourel, A. V.
1964. Method and Measurement in Sociology. New York: The Free Press of Glencoe.

Clark, Margaret
1972. Cultural Values and Dependency in Later Life. *In* Aging and

Modernization, Donald O. Cowgill and Lowell D. Holmes, eds. Pp. 263–74. New York: Appleton-Century-Crofts.

Clark, M. Margaret, and Barbara G. Anderson
1967. Culture and Aging: An Anthropological Study of Older Americans. Springfield, Ill.: Charles C Thomas.

Coe, Rodney
1965. Self Conception and Institutionalization. *In* Older People and Their Social World, Arnold Rose and Warren Peterson, eds. Pp. 225–43. Philadelphia: F.A. Davis.

Committee on Ways and Means
1976. National Health Insurance Resource Book. Rev. ed. Washington, D.C.: United States Government Printing Office.

Cook, Fay Lomax, et al.
1978. Criminal Victimization of the Elderly: The Physical and Economic Consequences. The Gerontologist 18:338–49.

Costello, J. P., and G. Tanaka
1961. Mortality and Morbidity in Long-Term Institutional Care of the Aged. Journal of the American Geriatric Society 9:959–63.

Cowgill, Donald C.
1974. The Aging of Populations and Societies. *In* Political Consequences of Aging, Frederick R. Eisele, ed. Pp. 1–18. Philadelphia: The American Academy of Political and Social Science.

Department of Health and Social Security
1974. Health and Personal Social Services Statistics for England. London: HMSO.

Department of Health and Social Security and Office of Population
1974. Censuses and Surveys.

Report on Hospital In-Patient Enquiry for the Year 1972. London: HMSO.

de Schweinitz, Karl
1943. England's Road to Social Security: From the Statute of Laborers in 1349 to the Beveridge Report of 1942. New York: A.S. Barnes and Company.

Dickson, J. F.
1976. Statement for the Hearings on Medical Appliances for the Elderly, Needs and Costs. Subcommittee on Health and Long-Term Care, Select Committee on Aging, House of Representatives.

Douglas, Jack D., ed.
1970. Understanding Everyday Life. Chicago: Aldine.

Dowd, James J.
1975. Aging as Exchange: A Preface to Theory. Journal of Gerontology 30:584:–95.

Ekeh, Peter P.
1974. Social Exchange Theory: The Two Traditions. Cambridge: Harvard University Press.

Emerson, Richard M.
1962. Power-Dependence Relations. American Sociological Review 27:31–41.

Estes, Carroll L.
1979. The Aging Enterprise. San Francisco: Jossey-Bass Publishers.

Exton-Smith, A. N., and H. Grimley Evans
1977. Care of the Elderly: Meeting the Challenge of Dependency. New York: Grune and Stratton.

Freymann, John Gordon, M.D.
1974. The American Health Care System: Its Genesis and Trajectory. New York: Medcom Inc.

Gilbert, Bentley B.
1966. The Evolution of National Insurance in Great Britain. London: Michael Joseph Limited.

Goldsmith, Jack, and Sharon S. Goldsmith
1976. Crime and the Elderly: An Overview. *In* Crime and the Elderly: Challenge and Response, Jack Goldsmith and Sharon S. Goldsmith, eds. Pp. 1–4 Lexington, Mass.: D.C. Heath and Company.

Gottesman, Leonard E.
1974. Nursing Home Performance as Related to Resident Traits,

Ownership, Size, and Source of Payment. American Journal of Public Health 64:269–76.

Gresham, M. L.
1976. The Infantilization of the Elderly: A Developing Concept. Nursing Forum 15:195–210.

Gunter, L. M.
1971. Students' Attitudes Toward Geriatric Nursing. Nursing Outlook 19:466–69.

Gubrium, Jaber F.
1975. Living and Dying at Murray Manor. New York: St. Martin's Press.

Halliburton, P. M., and W. B. Wright
1973. Variations in Standard of Hospital Geriatric Care. Lancet, 1:1300–02.

Henry, Jules
1963. Culture Against Man. New York: Random House.

1973. On Sham, Vulnerability and Other Forms of Self-Destruction. New York: Random House.

Hentig, Hans von
1948. The Criminal and His Victim. New Haven: Yale University Press.

Hickey, Tom
1980. Health and Aging. Monterey, Calif.: Brooks/Cole Pub. Co.

Homans, George C.
1961. Social Behavior: Its Elementary Forms. New York: Harcourt.

Howell, Trevor H.
1963. A Student's Guide to Geriatrics. Springfield, Ill.: Charles C Thomas.

Isaacs, Bernard, M. Livingstone, and Y. Neville
1972. Survival of the Unfittest: A Study of Geriatric Patients in Glasgow. London and Boston: Routledge and Kegan Paul.

Jaeger, Dorothea, and Leo W. Simmons
1970. The Aged Ill: Coping with Problems in Geriatric Care. New York: Appleton-Century-Crofts.

Kahana, Eva
1973. The Humane Treatment of Old People in Institutions. The Gerontologist 13:282–89.

Kahn, R. L., et al.
1960. Brief Objective Measure for the Determination of Mental Status in the Aged. American Journal of Psychiatry 117:326–28.

Kane, Robert L., and Roaslie A. Kane
1976. Long-Term Care in Six Countries: Implications for the United States. Washington, D.C.: U.S. Department of Health, Education, and Welfare. Public Health Service, National Institutes of Health, No. (NIH) 76–1207.

1978. Care of the Aged: Old Problems in Need of New Solutions. Science 200:913–19.

Kastenbaum, Robert J., and Sandra E. Candy
1973. The 4 Percent Fallacy: A Methodological and Empirical Critique of Extended Care Facility Program Statistics. International Journal of Aging and Human Development 4:15–21.

Kayser, Jeanie Schmit, and Fred A. Minnigerode
1975. Increasing Nursing Student's Interest in Working with Aged Patients. Nursing Research 24:23–26.

Kiefer, T. M.
1968. Institutionalized Friendship and Warfare Among the Tausug of Jolo. Ethnology 7:225–44.

Killian, Eldon C.
1970. Effect of Geriatric Transfers on Mortality Rates. Social Work 15:19–26.

Kosberg, J. I.
1973. Differences in Proprietary Institutions Caring for Affluent and Nonaffluent Elderly. The Gerontologist 13:299–304.

Kosberg, J. I., and S. S. Tobin
1972. Variability Among Nursing Homes. Gerontologist 12:2.

Leaf, Aleander
1973. Getting Old. Scientific American 22:45–52.

Markson, Elizabeth
1971. A Hiding Place to Die. Transaction/Society 9:48–54.

Mauss, Marcel
[1925]. The Gift: Forms and Functions of Exchange in Archaic Societies. Glencoe, Ill.: Free Press, 1954.

Mead, George Herbert
1934. Mind, Self and Society. Chicago: University of Chicago Press.

Mendelson, M. A.
1974. Tender Loving Greed. New York: Alfred A. Knopf.

Moss, Frank and Val J. Halamandaris
1977. Too Old, Too Sick, Too Bad: Nursing Homes in America. Germantown, Md.: Aspen Systems Corp.

Murray, David Stark
1974. Blueprint for Health. New York: Schocken.

Nursing Home Fact Book
1971. Washington, D.C.: American Nursing Home Association.

Office of Population Censuses and Surveys
1972. Census 1971: Preliminary Age and Sex Tables for Great Britain. London: HMSO.

1974. Census 1971 for Great Britain: Persons of Pensionable Age. London: HMSO.

1975. General Household Survey for 1972. London: HMSO.

Pelto, Pertti J.
1970. Anthropological Research: The Structure of Inquiry. New York: Harper and Row.

Pino, C. J., Lenore M. Rosica, and T. H. Carter
1978. The Differential Effects of Relocation on Nursing Home Patients. The Gerontologist 18:167–72.

Price, Sally
1978. Reciprocity and Social Distance: A Reconsideration. Ethnology 18:339–50.

Reif, Laura
1977. Community-Based In-Home Health Services: A Study of San Francisco's Two Non-Profit, Freestanding Home Health Agencies. Final Report of the San Francisco Foundation Project.

Reiman, Jeffrey H.
1976. Aging as Victimization: Reflections on the American Way of (Ending) Life. *In* Crime and the Elderly, Jack Goldsmith and Sharon S. Goldsmith, eds. Pp. 77–81. Lexington, Mass.: D.C. Heath and Company.

Report of the Working Party of the Royal College of Physicians at London
1977. Medical Care of the Elderly. Lancet 1:1092–95.

Rosen, George
1958. A History of Public Health. New York: MD Publications, Inc.

Rothman, David J.
1971. The Discovery of the Asylum: Social Order and Disorder in the New Republic. Boston: Little, Brown and Company.

Rubin, S. G., and G. H. Davies
1975. Bed Blocking by Elderly Patients in General Hospital Wards. Age and Ageing 4:142–47.

Sahlins, Marshall D.
1965. On the Sociology of Primitive Exchange. *In* the Relevance of Models for Social Anthropology, Michael Banton, ed. Pp. 139–236. New York: Praeger.

Schafer, Stephen
1977. Victimology: The Victim and His Criminal. Reston, Virginia: Reston Publishing Company.

Scull, Andrew T.
1977. Decarceration Community Treatment and the Deviant: A Radical View. Englewood Cliffs: Prentice-Hall.

Shanas, Ethel
1962. The Health of Older People: A Social Survey. Cambridge: Harvard University Press.

Shanas, Ethel, et al.
1968. Old People in Three Industrial Societies. New York: Atherton Press.

Shryock, Richard H.
1960. Medicine and Society in America: 1660–1860. Ithaca: Cornell University Press.

1966. Medicine in America: Historical Essays. Baltimore: The Johns Hopkins Press.

Siegel, Jacob S.
1978. Demographic Aspects of Aging and the Older Population in the United States. Current Population Reports. Special Studies, Series P-23, No. 59. Washington, D.C.: United States Bureau of the Census.

Simon, A., and R. B. Cahan
1963. The Acute Brain Syndrome in Geriatric Patients. *In* Acute Psychotic Reaction, W. M. Mendel and L. J. Epstein, eds. Washington, D.C.: Psychiatric Research Report No. 16. P. 8.

Special Committee on Aging, United States Senate
1972. Home Health Services in the United States. Washington, D.C.: United States Government Printing Office.

1974. Nursing Home Care in the United States. Failure in Public Policy. Prepared by the Subcommittee on Long-Term Care. Washington, D.C.: United States Government Printing Office.

Stevens, Rosemary
1966. Medical Practice in Modern England: The Impact of Specialization and State Medicine. New Haven: Yale University Press.

1971. American Medicine and the Public Interest. New Haven and London: Yale University Press.

Tiven, M. G.
1971. Older Americans: Special Handling Required. Washington, D.C.: National Council on the Aging.

Tobin, Sheldon S., and Morton A. Lieberman
1976. Last Home for the Aged. San Francisco: Jossey-Bass.

Townsend, Claire
1971. Old Age: The Last Segregation. New York: Grossman.

Townsend, Peter
1962. The Last Refuge. London: Routledge and Kegan Paul.

Townsend, P., and D. Wedderburn
1965. The Aged in the Welfare State. London: Bell.

United States Bureau of the Census
1973. General Population Characteristics, United States Summary. 1970 Census of Population. Washington, D.C.: United States Government Printing Office.

1975. Social and Economic Characteristics of the Older Population 1974. Current Population Reports, Special Studies, Series P-23, No. 57. Washington, D.C.: United States Government Printing Office.

1977. Projections of the Population of the United States, 1977–2050. Current Population Reports. Series P-25, No. 704. Washington, D.C.: United States Government Printing Office.

United States Congress, Congressional Budget Office
1977. Long-Term Care for the Elderly and Disabled. Washington, D.C.: United States Government Printing Office.

United States Department of Health, Education, and Welfare
1976. The British National Health Service: Conversations with Sir George E. Godber. Publication No. (NIH) 77–1205.

1977. Health—United States—1976–1977. No. (HRA) 77–1232. Hyattsville, Md.: National Center for Health Statistics.

Vail, David J.
1966. Dehumanization and the Institutional Career. Springfield, Ill.: Charles C Thomas

Walsh, John
1978. Federal Health Spending Passes the $50 Billion Mark. Science 200:886–87.

Wang, H. S.
1973. Special Diagnostic Procedures—The Evaluation of Brain Impair-

ment. *In* Mental Illness in Later Life, E.W. Busse and E. Pfeiffer, eds. Washington, D.C.: American Psychological Association.

Williamson, J., I. H. Stokoe, S. Gray, M. Fisher, A. Smith, A. McGhee, and E. Stephenson
1964. Old People at Home Their Unreported Needs. Lancet 1, 1117–20.

Whitemen, J.
1966. The Function of Food in Society. Nutrition 20:4–8.

Index